DISCARD

DATE DUE			

JUNE

CALLWOOD

a life of action

Anne Dublin

Library and Archives Canada Cataloguing in Publication

Dublin, Anne
June Callwood : a life of action / by Anne Dublin.

ISBN 1-897187-14-9
978-1-897187-14-2

1. Callwood, June—Juvenile literature. 2. Journalists—Canada—Biography—
Juvenile literature. 3. Human rights workers—Canada—Biography—-Juvenile
literature. 4. Authors, Canadian (English)—Biography—Juvenile literature.
I. Title.

PN4913.C34D82 2006   j070.92   C2006-903497-4

Edited by: Gena Gorrell
Designed by: Melissa Kaita

The author gratefully acknowledges the support of the Ontario Arts Council.

*Second Story Press gratefully acknowledges the support of the Ontario Arts Council and the
Canada Council for the Arts for our publishing program. We acknowledge the financial support
of the Government of Canada through the Book Publishing Industry Development Program,
and the Government of Ontario through the Ontario Media Development Corporation's
Ontario Book Initiative.*

Canada Council   Conseil des Arts
for the Arts   du Canada

ONTARIO ARTS COUNCIL
CONSEIL DES ARTS DE L'ONTARIO

Published by
SECOND STORY PRESS
20 Maud Street, Suite 401
Toronto, ON
M5V 2M5

www.secondstorypress.ca

For my beloved daughters—
Deborah, Sarah, and Miriam

CONTENTS

*"Each person is like a stone in a pond...
Individual actions, good or bad, send out tiny
ripples that change the surface of the public
pond. People, by choice, can spread warm
understanding or cold indifference."*

June Callwood

INTRODUCTION

WHO IS JUNE CALLWOOD? She's a journalist who has written newspaper and magazine articles about famous people like Terry Fox and Queen Elizabeth; she's also written about ordinary people caught up in extraordinary circumstances. She's tackled difficult subjects including child abuse, censorship, and prisons, as well as lighter subjects like the weather and the joys of flying. She's the author of 30 books on everything from the history of Canada, to human emotions, to one man's battle with AIDS.

June Callwood helped establish 50 organizations, including Digger House, for homeless youth; Nellie's Hostel for Women; Jessie's Centre for Teenagers; and Casey House, for people with AIDS. She's a Companion of the Order of Canada, the highest honor the country can bestow upon its citizens. She has a street named after her, and a park, too.

June Callwood has experienced controversy and tragedy in her own life, but has managed to keep going in spite of her problems. She has helped the homeless, the poor, the hopeless, and the dying. She has been called "master of the art of hope."

chapter 1
COUNTRY GIRL

JUNE ROSE CALLWOOD WAS BORN ON JUNE 2, 1924, in the small town of Chatham, in southwestern Ontario. Her parents were Gladys Lavoie and Harold (Byng) Callwood. The Lavoies were of French descent, and had settled in Quebec City in 1650; the Callwoods's ancestors had been British.

Gladys Lavoie had a hard life at first. Her mother, Dorcas, died when Gladys was a toddler. Her father, William (Bill) Lavoie, remarried, and eventually Gladys was sent to a convent school—a Catholic school run by nuns—in Montreal. She hated that school. When she was just 16, handsome Byng Callwood came along and Gladys ran away with him to get married. Byng was 20 years old. This "mixed marriage" between

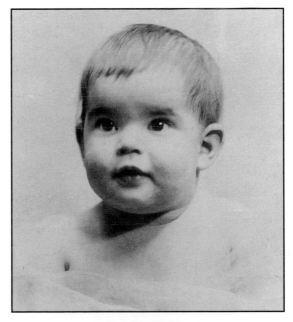

June, one year old

an Anglican and a Catholic was scandalous at that time. How would the young couple support themselves? Where would they live so that they would both be accepted?

Byng and Gladys lived in the town of Tilbury, where Byng's parents had their home. When June was two years old, they moved west to Belle River, a French-Canadian village of 800 people, close to Detroit. Belle River was the home of Gladys's father and her stepmother, Rose.

Byng Callwood, June's father

A plumber by trade, Byng Callwood was a clever man. He built a tinning plant down by the bridge in Belle River and named it the Superior Tinning and Retinning Company. Gladys and Byng repaired tin milk cans that dairy farmers brought them, but it was hard, dirty work. They often burned their arms on the melting, splattering tin. No wonder neither of them liked it!

June's younger sister, Jane, was born in 1927. Jane had a lot of ear infections when she was young. In addition, she had dyslexia, a condition that makes it harder to learn to read. In those days, most teachers didn't know about dyslexia or how to help children like Jane.

Gladys Lavoie always wanted a better life for herself and her daughters. Although she spoke French to June when she was young, Gladys worked hard to learn English, since she believed English would help them get ahead. Gladys sent June to piano lessons with the nuns in Belle River and to dance lessons in Windsor.

Gladys wasn't afraid to fight for her beliefs. One time, she argued with a priest because she wanted to dress June in ankle socks like the American kids just across the border. But the priest said that respectable

Gladys with her daughters, June and Jane

young ladies didn't allow anyone to see their legs, and that June should continue to wear full-length stockings. It was 1930, and June was only six years old.

In Belle River, a village only ten blocks long, life moved at a much slower pace than it does now. Some summer nights, June played "Hide and Seek" with Jane and her sister's young friends. Mostly, though, June played on her own. As she says, "I was a loner who lived in my imagination." June liked to play dress-up in her grandfather Lavoie's attic and to pretend that

June and Jane

she lived in a huge mansion. Jane, being younger and less adventurous, was much more protected than June. That arrangement suited both of the girls just fine. June had a lot of freedom, and she learned to become strong and independent, just like her mother.

But the girls weren't really alone. Everyone knew everyone else in Belle River, and helped if someone was in trouble. Grown-ups always knew where June was supposed to be, and would give her help or advice if she needed it. In the winter twilight, June walked home alone from piano lessons at the convent. If she ever fell down, a friendly neighbor would pick her up, wipe her tears, and make sure she was all right before sending her on her way.

From 1920 to 1933, the United States had "Prohibition" laws that made it illegal to manufacture or sell alcoholic drinks. Some Americans smuggled liquor across the border from Canada, and others made their own—sometimes in the bathtub!

June's grandfather Bill Lavoie was living near the American border, and he began sneaking liquor into the United States via the Detroit River. He made a lot of money, and built an imposing stone house on Notre Dame Street in Belle River. Next door to his house, he owned a beautiful restaurant. Prohibition was also in effect in Ontario for part of the 1920s, and the restaurant concealed a "speakeasy," a place where customers drank liquor illegally.

While June and her family lived in Belle River, she often visited Grandfather Bill at his restaurant. He was a quiet man whose presence comforted her. A crippling disease had left him unable to walk, and June would lean against his wheelchair and watch him while he played solitaire for hours at a time.

June's other grandfather, Harold Callwood, was a magistrate for Essex and Kent counties in the town of Tilbury. Everyone called him Judge Callwood. He was a large, kindly man. On summer days, young June liked to sit on the verandah while Judge Callwood listened to cases that were brought before him.

Most women who worked outside the home in the 1920s were secretaries, store clerks, or factory workers. Few could enter professions like law, medicine, or engineering. After all, it was only in 1918 that women were allowed to vote in federal elections in Canada. Up until 1929, they could not be members of Canada's Senate in Ottawa, because the law did not define them as "persons." But Grandfather Callwood was proud of June and felt she could achieve a great deal. He even put aside money in his will so that she could go to law school—something almost unheard of for a girl at that time. His belief in June encouraged her, and she dreamed of becoming a lawyer or a doctor.

And what about June's grandmothers? Margaret Anne Callwood was beloved in the town of Tilbury. She was active in a women's charitable organization called the Imperial Order Daughters of the Empire (IODE). Rose Lavoie, in Belle River, was petite, shy, and deeply religious.

But both women had plenty of responsibility. This was well before convenience foods and electrical appliances became part of everyday life, a time when women had to do their cooking "from scratch." They also did most of their housework by hand, without washing machines, vacuum cleaners, refrigerators, irons, or toasters. They worked hard cooking meals, baking bread and cakes, scrubbing floors, and dusting furniture.

When they went out, June's grandmothers liked to wear pretty dresses and fancy hats. They enjoyed playing cards with other ladies, and on Sundays they attended church (Roman Catholic or Anglican, depending on the grandmother). Sometimes, when Grandmother Callwood's friends came to visit in the summer while June was there, June served them little iced cakes she had helped bake in her grandmother's kitchen. She still remembers the flowered oilcloth on the table.

When June was young in Belle River, the family had electricity and, after a while, indoor plumbing. The house was heated

The Belle River home of June's Lavoie grandparents

Gladys Lavoie Callwood, June's mother

by a wood-burning stove in the kitchen. In the winter, pipes were attached to the stove to send heat to the second floor. There were a lot of cold corners in that house.

One of June's best friends was Nanny Garber. Nanny's parents owned a dress shop near Grandfather Bill's restaurant. Most of the people in Belle River acted coolly toward the Garber family. Maybe it was because they were the only Jewish people in that French-Canadian, Catholic village. But June didn't feel completely accepted either, because her father was English and Anglican. June and Nanny played together, pretending they were outcasts, alone and friendless in the world.

June also made friends with a Chinese man who was the cook in her grandfather's restaurant. They sometimes placed two straight chairs on the sidewalk in front of the restaurant and sat watching the passing cars and farmers' wagons. He taught her how to say her name and a few other words in Chinese.

The cook often showed June a faded picture of his wife and two small children in faraway China. When he looked at the photo, he would cry. Although June didn't know it at the time, in 1923 the Canadian government had passed a law that banned all but a few Chinese immigrants from entering Canada. The lonely man probably believed he would never see his wife and children again.

Besides playing with Nanny and talking with the cook, in the summer June liked to go to the tomato cannery and visit the farmers while they stood in line to get their wagons, loaded with tomatoes, weighed. She would sit on the high seat of an open wagon and eat tomatoes still warm from the fields, while she watched the horses munching their oats. On hot summer nights, she liked to climb the cherry tree behind her house and gaze at the stars for hours.

When she was old enough, June attended Belle River's brick Separate School. When her teachers saw that she could read, write, and do arithmetic, she skipped three grades at once. This gave her the chance to learn a lot more—but it also meant that she was much younger than the other children in her grade.

June's elementary school graduating class. June, age 12, is third from the right in the front row.

The Kitchener swim team, 1936. June is third from left.

In 1929 the economy collapsed and the country sank into the Great Depression. Many companies went out of business. In 1934 the Superior Tinning and Retinning Company failed. June's family moved to Kitchener, a large town about 250 kilometers (150 miles) east of Belle River. At first they lived in a small apartment over a downtown store.

June went to Victoria Public School, where Mr. J.F. Carmichael, the principal and June's English teacher, taught her grammar and helped her to develop her writing skills. Even more important, he helped her gain confidence in her abilities. Because she was so much younger than her classmates, June sometimes felt left out of their games. When she was lonely, she'd read a book and forget about her troubles for a while.

Another activity June loved was swimming and diving. When she was about 11 years old, she was on the Kitchener swim team. Another girl, Dorothy Schaeffer, could do diving somersaults that June hadn't mastered yet. Dorothy and June were always competing against each other.

One day, Dorothy dived poorly and hit the water with a loud belly flop. Without thinking, June cried out, "Oh, good!" A boy sitting beside her on the bench turned to her and said in a low voice, "That wasn't kind." At once, June felt ashamed of her nasty comment. She recalls, "Drenched in shame, I discovered in that instant that I wanted to be a nice person a whole lot more than I wanted to win a ribbon." She decided she would treat people with more consideration from that day on.

When June was 12, her parents sent her to boarding school—Notre Dame Academy, in Waterdown, near Hamilton, about an hour's drive from home.

She lived at the school and came home only for Christmas. Why did June's parents send her away to school? Jane had a lot of ear infections and Gladys needed to spend more time taking care of her. In addition, Gladys wanted June to learn skills like sewing and baking, besides her regular schoolwork. She even hoped June would learn to act more like a "lady."

June didn't mind at all, for she felt strongly attracted to the Catholic faith. She liked everything about being Catholic—the Latin prayers, the incense, the long dresses the nuns wore, and the beauty and peace of the chapel. She decided that she wanted to become a nun.

Notre Dame Academy

chapter 2

TROUBLED TIMES

AS IT TURNED OUT, June stayed at the convent for only one year. The world was still sunk in the depths of the Great Depression, and the 1930s became known as the "Dirty Thirties." People all over Canada were in dire straits. By 1936, more than 1.5 million Canadians (about 14 percent) were unemployed and receiving government "relief" payments. Back then, people didn't get enough unemployment insurance to tide them over until things got better. Many felt that accepting handouts, no matter what they were called, was humiliating and disheartening.

By 1937 June's parents couldn't afford to pay her school fees any longer, so June had to return home. At first she felt disappointed about leaving Notre Dame, but she soon adjusted to the more exciting life outside the convent walls. Besides, she had missed her family.

Gladys had missed June, too. The first thing she did when June came home was to throw out June's Bible, her rosary, and her prayer cards. She'd had enough of her daughter wanting to become a nun.

But Byng still couldn't make enough money to support the family. In 1937, when his debts became overwhelming, he left Gladys and his two young daughters to become one of thousands of men who went out west to look for work. All he could find was a job threshing wheat on prairie farms during harvest time, for a dollar a day.

After Byng left the family, things went from bad to worse. Gladys and the girls became desperately poor. Sometimes they couldn't afford to pay the rent, and were forced to move from one house to another in the middle of the night. At other times, the sheriff took their furniture as payment for the rent they owed. Because she was younger and would get more sympathy, Jane was often the one who went to the store to ask the shopkeeper for a loaf of bread or a bottle of milk, or one more can of pork and beans. She would promise to pay for them later.

In 1937 June was in grade 10. She was 13—an age when girls are self-conscious about their clothes and appearance, and sensitive to their status among other girls. She didn't want anyone to know when she hadn't eaten for days. She felt embarrassed to wear cast-off clothes that might have belonged to a classmate.

Because she had skipped three grades and was so much younger than the rest of her class, June didn't fit in, and often felt awkward in social situations. For example, once when she was in her teens, a friend invited her over for tea and asked if she wanted it with milk or with lemon. June had never been offered tea before and she wasn't sure what to answer, so she said, "Both." The lemon made the milk curdle, and June wanted to sink through the floor.

June never forgot how it felt to be poor. In later years she remembered, "It all flooded back how it hurts to see people eating when you haven't eaten for a day, or two, or three... For the rest of your life, you feel

June, age 16

that everything you have can be taken away from you and you can be hungry again."

But she was resilient, and she found a way to help herself feel better. In one house where they lived, there was an open porch off her bedroom. When June couldn't sleep, she pulled a mattress out onto the porch, lay down on her back, and watched the "black, fathomless sky" where "millions, trillions of stars sparkled with icy light... On nights I could see the stars, I was never lonely or lost."

June also escaped into books. Like many young people who grow up to be writers, she was a voracious reader. Her aim was to read every book from A to Z in the entire Kitchener public library. She took out five books every day, glanced through the ones she didn't find interesting, and ended up reading about two books a day. Over time, she reached her goal and worked her way through the whole library.

With Byng gone, Gladys was desperate to find work to support the family. She was able to earn some money as a seamstress. June remembers her "sewing hundreds of tiny sequins, one at a time, on someone's party dress." Although her life was difficult, Gladys was loyal, and never spoke badly of her husband after he left the family.

The Depression was a dreadful time for many people, but worse was still to come. World War II began in September 1939, when Germany invaded Poland. With country after country in Europe falling to the German forces in Hitler's *blitzkrieg* (lightning war), the "Allied" forces of Britain and the Commonwealth countries, and later the United States, were left to fight the "Axis" forces—Germany, Italy, and later Japan. In the first month of the war, over fifty thousand men joined the Canadian army, and thousands more joined the navy, air force, and merchant marine.

Byng Callwood signed up in 1939 with the Royal Canadian Engineers (RCE). Being an army engineer was a job that suited him well because of his previous work experience.

Among other arduous and dangerous tasks, the RCE built or repaired bridges and roads to help the Allied soldiers invade Europe, notably on two fronts—Italy and France. They built airfields, set up anti-tank obstacles, and laid and cleared away explosives.

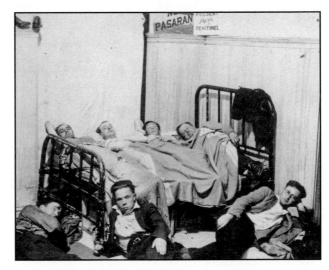

In the Depression, June's father was one of thousands of men who traveled far from home in search of a job. Living conditions for these men were often very poor.

Byng Callwood was a member of the Royal Canadian Engineers, who built this bridge near Vaucelles, France, in just eight days.

Without the work of the RCE, the soldiers would not have been able to advance and thus eventually win the war.

Gladys and the girls joined Byng for a year in Regina, Saskatchewan, where he trained before going overseas in 1940. June loved Regina and had a great time at Centre Collegiate Institute.

Byng stayed with the RCE until the war ended in 1945. During the relentless bombing of London, England (1940–1941), he worked in a bomb-disposal squad where he defused unexploded bombs that German planes had dropped on the city. One veteran of the Royal Canadian Air Force (RCAF) has said, "The guys in the bomb-disposal squad had to have nerves of steel and be a little crazy." Byng worked heroically, and did well in the RCE. But he rarely wrote home.

A famous symbol of the Great Depression, the "Bennett buggy." When people could no longer afford gas for their cars, they reverted to old-fashioned horsepower to pull them, and named the combination after the prime minister of the time, R. B. Bennett, whose policies many people blamed for the Depression.

After Byng went overseas in 1940, Gladys and the girls moved back to Ontario and settled in Brantford—the town where Alexander Graham Bell made the first long-distance phone call in 1876, and where hockey superstar Wayne Gretzky would be born in 1961.

At last, June had found a setting where she felt comfortable. She began to make friends in Brantford. CBC producer Ross McLean, who went to high school with her, remembered her like this: "June was unlike anyone we had known before, a definite original. Her beauty and her openness caught our fancy, for sure, but so did her unconventional ways."

Because she liked to read and write, June was on the staff of Brantford Collegiate's school magazine. Back in Kitchener, she had also worked on Kitchener Collegiate's school newspaper, *The Grumbler*, and had written a weekly column about high school news for the *Kitchener Record*.

June was such a good writer that she won a short-story contest. A man called Judge Sweet gave her the award and told her to see him if she ever needed a job. When June was 16 and in her fourth year of high school, Gladys forced her to quit school in order to help support the family. June promptly went to see Judge Sweet. He was as good as his word. He was on the board of directors of the local newspaper, *The Brantford Expositor*, and he gave her a letter of introduction to the publisher.

June was hired for a six-day week, fifteen hours per day. She earned a total of $7.50 for the week. Half of this small sum she handed over to her mother for rent. From her first paycheck, she bought a pair of high-heeled shoes for two dollars. They didn't fit properly and made her feet bleed. She couldn't return them, so she packed them with Kleenex and kept wearing them.

June, at about age 18, in Brantford

At that time, June didn't have any great ambition to become a writer. She just needed a job. She later said she was hired by *The Brantford Expositor* because so many men were away fighting in the war. That may have been the reason she got the job, but that's not why she kept it. She would prove her worth in no time at all.

It was the bitterly cold month of February 1941. The Depression was finally over, and thousands of jobs—for men and women—became available, not only in the military but in shipyards, iron foundries, aircraft plants, and engineering shops. All of Canada was gearing up to make airplanes, ships, and supplies for the war effort. There was no shortage of jobs now, but some foods became scarce, as products like butter, sugar, tea, and coffee were rationed, and only so much was doled out to each family.

The war dragged on and the Allies suffered one painful defeat after another. The Battle of the Atlantic, the Battle of Britain, the Dieppe

Raid—these were the names people heard on the radio or read in the newspaper, with worry in their hearts.

A Speed Graphic camera, the kind June used in her early days as a reporter

Back home in Brantford, June had established a routine. Every morning at 7:30, she bought a chocolate bar and a Coke (breakfast) for ten cents at the newsstand across from her office. Then she started her day at the *Expositor*.

At first, she didn't even work at a proper desk; she wrote her stories on an old manual Underwood typewriter perched on a table. During the morning she was a proofreader; she checked other reporters's writing for grammar and spelling mistakes (although she says she still can't spell very well). In the afternoon she wrote stories about the soldiers at the local army camp and the air force flying school near Brantford. A lot of soldiers fell in love with the pretty reporter, and even wrote letters to her when they went overseas. June took photos with a Speed Graphic camera, but she didn't get very good pictures until she learned to keep the camera centered on the subject when she pressed the shutter. She was learning the essential skills of a journalist—research and writing, and how to work to a deadline.

Five nights a week, she ate a chopped chicken sandwich on toast and drank another Coke at the Olympia Restaurant near the office. Mr. Vlachos, the owner of the restaurant, was worried that she was too thin and sometimes gave her a free meal. Then, in the evening, June edited country news written by local people, about meetings and social events, county fairs and church socials. She didn't sleep much or eat well, but she had never felt better in her life.

In those days, the typical woman reporter was like Miss Ethel Raymond, who worked at the paper. June once said, "Miss Raymond was a perfect character. She wore gloves and I think sometimes typed with them on, and she always kept her hat on in the office. She was a stoutly corseted woman who couldn't spell..."

June made friends with the other female news reporter, Isobel Plant. They were both young and pretty, and people started calling them the "paper dolls."

People at the *Expositor* still talk about June Callwood. When she paid the office a visit in 2001, they crowded around her and said they were proud she had started out at their paper. After all, this was where she practiced and improved the skills that would eventually make her a top-rate journalist.

But *The Brantford Expositor* was only the beginning. In 1942, the city editor of the *Toronto Daily Star* asked June to come and work for his newspaper. She was thrilled—especially because he offered her twenty-five dollars a week, much more than she was getting at the *Expositor*. June knew only one person in Toronto, but that didn't stop her. She looked forward to the exciting life in the big city, and to being on her own.

chapter 3
JUNE CALLWOOD, GIRL REPORTER

IT WAS SEPTEMBER OF 1942 and June couldn't wait to begin her new job as a reporter for the *Toronto Daily Star*. She wore her high-heeled shoes to make herself look older. However, when the city editor saw her in person, he decided that she looked much too young to be a reporter. He demoted her to secretary, right there on the spot.

As part of June's new duties, she wrote the captions under photographs, measured them to be sure they fit, and answered the mail. She wasn't happy with these tedious tasks, since she'd been doing much more interesting work at the *Expositor*. However, she decided she should take what she could get for the time being.

What she got, though, was trouble. An army sergeant at Camp Borden wrote to the editor and criticized a caption June had written about an army tank. The angry letter was passed down to June to handle. She wrote back and said she was amazed that sergeants could read at all. (Byng Callwood was a sergeant by then, and June thought the man would understand the joke. He didn't.) The sergeant complained about June to her editor. Her boss told her that she should have shown more respect to a soldier, and he fired her immediately. She had held the job for just two weeks.

Stunned to find herself unemployed, June went to the *Toronto Telegram* and asked if they needed any reporters. They gave her an application for a secretarial job. But June didn't want to be a secretary again; she yearned to be a news reporter. And yet she knew she couldn't go back to Brantford. After all, they had given her a going-away party and everybody had wished her well. She was too embarrassed to tell them how quickly she had lost her job at the big-city newspaper.

June had a brilliant idea—she would enlist in the RCAF, to fight in the war that was still raging overseas. She wanted to fly a fighter plane. But her excitement turned to disappointment when she was informed at

World War II recruiting drives, like this one in an Eaton's window, showed women in new roles.

the recruiting office that the RCAF Women's Division did not train pilots. Women were allowed to work only as drivers, mechanics, secretaries, nurses, or cooks. But if June couldn't fly, she didn't want to be in the air force at all.

In desperation, she went to the *Globe and Mail* building at King and York Streets. But to whom should she speak? She asked the elevator man the name of the managing editor. He told her that it was Mr. Bob Farquharson, and that his office was on the fifth floor. June walked straight into Mr. Farquharson's office. If the secretary had been there, she wouldn't have been allowed in, but fortunately the secretary had gone for lunch.

Farquharson was seated behind his desk at one end of his long office. He looked at 18-year-old June and said, "You look like you're looking for a job." June explained that she'd had experience writing for *The Brantford Expositor*. She knew he must be desperate for reporters, since so many men were in the armed forces. Farquharson decided to give her a three-day trial.

June's first assignment was to write about a convention of the Ontario Medical Association at the elegant Royal York Hotel in downtown Toronto. When she entered the grand lobby, with its crystal chandeliers and ornate furnishings, she was dumbfounded. There were over a thousand rooms in the hotel, and many different sessions were taking place in different rooms, all at once. How could she cover everything?

June stumbled about until Don Carlson, a reporter from the *Star*, took pity on her and helped her figure out what to do. He didn't even seem to mind that her story appeared first, since the *Globe and Mail* was a morn-

At home, women worked in munitions factories soldering
flare tubes (above) and fuse boxes (below).

ing paper and the *Star* came out in the afternoon. Much to June's relief, Farquharson decided to hire her as a staff reporter after that.

June was given a variety of assignments. Once she filled in for the drama critic, who was ill. She was supposed to review a play at the Royal Alexandra Theatre. But June had never seen a play before in her life. How would she know if this one was good or bad?

June also covered the courts, but she got into trouble when she naively revealed some facts about a drug case that was still going on. How did this young reporter find out the secrets? She interviewed the key prosecution witness while she and the witness were in the ladies' room! June learned that the woman was a drug addict, and the police were supplying her with heroin so that she could testify. The paper printed June's article. Because the key witness's testimony was tainted by this bribery, the case was overturned and the 18 accused men were released.

June sometimes interviewed wounded soldiers returning from the war in Europe. Here's an excerpt from an article she wrote in August 1944, when the war had been dragging on for five grim years: "It took a Canadian pilot one hour and 58 minutes to get from his base in England to a spot over a certain occupied country. It took eight weeks for him to return to British soil—on foot." The pilot, Bob Clements, had been shot down over France, which was under German control, in November of 1943. He had bailed out 30 seconds before the burning plane exploded. After three days, hungry and disoriented, Clements had gotten help from the secret resistance fighters of the French Underground. They had eventually led him down to Gibraltar, then north to Britain, and from there he had finally returned home to Canada.

June soon settled into some regular assignments: Board of Education meetings, the Miss Toronto pageant, the Kiwanis Music Festival, and department store fashion shows in spring and fall. Her vivid, lively writing captured the tastes and interests of the times. About women's fashions, she wrote: "In the manner of the old fox who disdained the grapes he couldn't reach, Canadian women are consoling themselves with a current rumor that New York clothes are no good anyway." Covering teen styles, she noted:

Fashions for the algebra and fudge sundae set were displayed yesterday at a Junior Vogue show in Simpson's, and the predominant note for 1946 seems to be that shirttails should be tucked firmly in and bobby socks dismissed altogether.

June loved everything about Toronto—especially working for an important newspaper, and earning a good salary after all those years of poverty. She bought a new pair of shoes for $12—quite a bit of money in those days. For the first time in two years, she had a pair of comfortable shoes to wear.

There were other changes in June's life around that time. When she had first moved to Toronto, she shared a two-bedroom apartment with three other young women, and after that she lived in a couple of rooming houses. Then, in the autumn of 1943, Gladys and Jane moved to Toronto, where

Jane went to Oakwood Collegiate for her last two years of high school. June lived with them for a time in a one-bedroom basement apartment.

June was making friends with her fellow reporters. One was Bobbie Rosenfeld, female former Olympic track-and-field star who wrote a daily column called "Sports Reel." June recalls Bobbie with fondness:

> I was still in my teens and needed a mentor but all the other women reporters were in the women's department and seemed preoccupied with weddings and fashion, which didn't interest me. But there was Bobbie—somewhat salty, down-to-earth, funny, and very smart... She took me under her wing.

Other reporters also gave June a lot of help in those early days. For example, they showed her how to write a powerful "lead," the first paragraph of a news story that tells the basic facts—who, where, and when—and makes you curious to read the rest. June was successful partly because people helped her—but they also helped her because she was June. Journalist Susan Crean summed it up:

Bobbie Rosenfeld

She made it because she was clever, absorbing the lessons as fast as they came, and because she ran into some generous souls who saved her bacon more than once. Perhaps it was out of concern for an 18-year-old kid alone in the big city; perhaps it was Callwood's sunny nature.

June wrote in a breezy, chatty style, as if she were talking to her readers in person. They always came away knowing more than they had before.

But soon her writing would take second place behind another stage in her life.

Lunenburg, Nova Scotia, on assignment for CBC television

chapter 4

PARTNERS FOREVER

TRENT GARDINER FRAYNE WAS BORN ON SEPTEMBER 13, 1918, in Brandon, Manitoba. He was nicknamed "Billy" and he would go by that name for 24 years, until he moved to Toronto. His oldest friends still call him Bill; other friends call him Trent or Frayne.

Trent grew up poor, as did many people during the Depression. His mother, Ella, like most women of her era, had to be frugal to make ends meet. She knew how to cook and bake and knit. Trent describes his early life like this:

> I was an only child growing up in a one-bedroom apartment, sleeping on a pull-out couch in the living room. I was raised by a father who was away a lot and a mother who was the oldest girl in a family of 10 children... When I was a boy in Brandon, we were poor in the way that most of the people we knew were poor in those days, but my mother was ingenious at stretching our income and we were never hungry. I remember, for instance, that she used to add bread cubes to stretch a pan of fried potatoes. For years I thought that was the way you cooked fried potatoes.

Trent's father, Homer, worked for the Canadian Pacific Railway (CPR) as a brakeman and later as a conductor. He was a tall, blue-eyed, outgoing man who told wonderful stories, and was a good singer, too. To supplement the family income, Homer played poker. One of his card games could last all night, or even for three or four days. But Homer was skillful at the game, and he won most of the time.

When Trent was young, he played a lot of sports—hockey, basketball, baseball, and tennis. In high school and later at Brandon College, he wrote about sports for the local paper, the *Brandon Sun*. In his memoirs he talks about the beginning of his career:

> I had to write my copy before I went to school in the morning, so I'd set the alarm for 5 a.m. and go into the bathroom and close the door to avoid waking my parents. I'd perch on the throne, next to which was a small radiator with a wooden cover where my mother would pile towels and facecloths. I'd move them off and use the radiator cover for a desk. I'd write my copy with a thick black pencil, hike down to the *Sun* and drop it through the letter slot, then continue on to school.

During his long career as a sportswriter, Trent wrote articles for the *Winnipeg Tribune*, the Canadian Press News Service, and the *Globe and Mail*, as well as magazines like *Maclean's*, the *Saturday Evening Post*, and *Sports Illustrated*. He wrote 14 books and covered many of the world's major sporting events, including the Olympics, the Kentucky Derby, and the Super Bowl.

He received many honors and awards, including the 1997 Achievement Award from Sports Media Canada.

Other journalists admired Trent's writing. Pierre Berton, one of Canada's best-known authors and journalists, called him "likely Canada's greatest sportswriter ever." Jack Batten, a good friend and fellow sportswriter, says, "He builds humor into it and addresses the reader at the middle distance... I'd recognize a Frayne piece anytime."

June and Trent, 1943

Here's a taste of Trent's writing, from 1999:

The millennium beckons. Soon sports scribes will stagger under an irrepressible urge to crown Canada's greatest athlete of the century. Restless brains will cogitate, meditate and deliberate. Who was the greater, Howie Morenz or Bobby

June and Trent at the *Globe and Mail* in 1943

Orr? Gordie Howe or Jean Beliveau? Cyclone Taylor or Rocket Richard? Or will the nowadays hero, Wayne What'shisname, head all the rest?

Trent was working for the *Globe and Mail* when June arrived fresh from her stint at the *Expositor*. She had read one of his articles while she was still in Brantford and had thought, "He's a lovely-looking person and, boy, can he write!" He seemed like someone she would like to get to know. So when she came to the *Globe and Mail*, she asked where Trent's desk was. She found that he was a calm man with a wonderful sense of humor. He thought she was "gorgeous, long-legged and sweet, flighty too, a beauty with a perfect quarter-moon smile." It was love at first sight.

At first, they went out casually with other reporters after work. But pretty soon they drifted together and became a couple. One night when they were having dinner together in the apartment June shared with

June in 1942 when she joined the staff of the *Globe and Mail*

Gladys and Jane, Trent found himself proposing marriage. He was surprised and she was delighted.

A week before the wedding, Trent said, "Honey, if you want to get out of this, I'll understand." June answered, "Buster, not a chance!"

June and Trent were married in St. Thomas's Anglican Church, in Toronto, on May 13, 1944. Bob Farquharson, the *Globe and Mail*'s managing editor, walked June down the aisle and gave her away. (The war was not over yet, and Byng was still overseas in the RCE.) Ralph Hyman and Frank Tumpane, two other reporters, were ushers; Jane was the bridesmaid; and Don Cannon, a friend of Trent's from Brandon, was the best man. Fittingly, the reception was at the Royal York Hotel, the scene of June's first assignment for the *Globe and Mail*. June wore a gray flannel suit, a white hat, and her $12 pair of good shoes. She still remembers the scent of the gardenias in her bouquet.

Sergeant and Mrs. Harold Callwood
announce the marriage of their daughter
June
to
Mr. Trent Frayne
on Saturday, May the thirteenth
nineteen hundred and forty-four
St. Thomas' Anglican Church
Toronto

June and Trent's wedding invitation, 1944

The next month, the couple went by train to Clear Lake, Manitoba, for their honeymoon. Trent had loved going there when he was a boy and wanted to visit the place again. It was early in the season and most of the resort where they were staying was closed. When Trent went out to run an errand, June slipped on her bathing suit, ran down to the dock, and dived into the lake. She has never forgotten the shock of the icy water!

It was wartime, and the couple received practical gifts. The publisher of the *Globe and Mail*, George McCullagh, gave them a dining-room table and chairs; Byng sent money from overseas to buy dishes; and other people gave them sheets, an end table, and a lamp. June and Trent were grateful for all their wedding gifts.

When June and Trent got married, June didn't change her name to Frayne, because the *Globe and Mail* didn't allow a married couple to be on staff at the same time. Besides, back then a lot of people thought a woman should stay at home if her husband had a job. Bob Farquharson asked June to keep the Callwood byline. (The "byline" is the *line* of print saying whom the story is written *by*.) She was so good at her job by then that, rules or no rules, he didn't want to lose her.

Later, after June left the *Globe and Mail*, she and Trent became known as Canada's husband-and-wife freelance writing team. Between the two of them, they wrote hundreds of articles for magazines and newspapers. They talked about their work and asked each other for feedback. They helped each other with problems and they often laughed and joked about what they'd written. They took two typewriters with them whenever they went on vacation.

June and Trent

What does it mean to work "freelance?" The term comes from the Middle Ages, when knights were obliged to use their swords and lances to defend one particular nobleman and his land. However, a few men had a "free lance" and could hire themselves out to work for whomever they wanted. That was how June wanted to work—deciding for herself what to write about and for whom.

Although June was working at an unconventional job, she had one thing in common with other women of her time—her husband, family, and home were always her top priority. After her turbulent teenage years, a solid marriage gave her the strength and security she needed to develop her writing talents further, and to pursue her other interests. She later wrote, "Because of the family bond, I am free of the fear of failure or fall from dignity that immobilizes many people; I am absolutely safe."

chapter 5
SPREADING HER WINGS

MUCH AS JUNE ENJOYED HER JOB, she quit the *Globe and Mail* in 1945. She and Trent were expecting their first child. They had a little girl that same year, and named her Jill.

In 1945, World War II ended and soldiers flocked home to Canada as quickly as they could. Byng Callwood was one of them. However, by that time Gladys had decided that their marriage was over. She stayed in Toronto and Byng moved to Winnipeg, where he went on to invent a machine for eviscerating (gutting) chickens. He made a fortune in the poultry business, and people called him the "Poultry King."

Although June loved being home with Jill, she soon started to feel restless. Ever since she had interviewed young men at the flying school near Brantford, she had wanted to learn to fly. Now was her chance.

June found the perfect teacher in Violet Milstead. Violet had joined the Royal Air Transport Auxiliary (RATA) in 1943. She had been one of only four Canadian women in the RATA. Since women weren't allowed to fly in combat, Violet's job had been to fly unarmed planes to wherever they were needed. For example, she flew planes from the factory in Canada to air-force fields in Britain. Violet was a slim, petite woman, but she piloted many

Violet Milstead in 2000, with her most famous flying student

different kinds of planes, from single-engine trainers to seaplanes to four-engine aircraft—over 45 different types in all. She never let anything stop her.

In 1946, June took flying lessons with Violet at Barker Field, on the outskirts of Toronto. While Jill amused herself in her playpen in the control tower, her mother was up in the skies, earning a pilot's license.

June loved flying. She loved the feeling of peace as she flew up into the sky, away from life's troubles. However, one evening as dusk was falling, she had trouble seeing some power lines and only narrowly avoided them. If she had run into them, she could have been badly injured or killed. That experience shook her up. Jill was still very young, and June was expecting a second child. As soon as she landed, she decided never to pilot a plane again.

June was so impressed with her remarkable flying teacher that she wrote an article about her. It was published in *Liberty* magazine in 1946, and June was paid the grand sum of $50. In June 1947, she wrote her first article for *Maclean's* magazine. In "Bell's Sweet Singers," June described an amateur women's choir called the Leslie Bell Singers: "Two nights a week, 40 weeks a year, 60 charming and lively young ladies voluntarily gather in the Ontario College of Education on Toronto's Bloor Street to be insulted." She had made the jump—she was now a freelance writer.

During her career, June would write approximately 1,500 articles for popular magazines like *Maclean's*, *Chatelaine*, and *Canadian Living*. Most of the time, the managing editor of a magazine—perhaps Ralph Allen from *Maclean's* or Doris Anderson from *Chatelaine*—would phone her and ask her to write an article. June was interested in everything and loved to learn about new things. She would go to the library and spend hours reading up on the subject she was writing about. She also interviewed people to get various "angles" or perspectives on the topic. But she always had her own style and point of view.

In 1951, June and Trent scraped together the down payment for a "quirky, funny old house" on the outskirts of Toronto. By then they felt crowded in their two-bedroom apartment, for they had three children: Jill was six; their second child, Brant (nicknamed Barney), was three; and Jennifer (later changed to Jesse) was still a baby. June loved having children. She once said, "I would have had a baby a year... They're full of God if God is goodness and decency and capacity for affection."

The house was not much bigger than their old apartment. It had only one small heater, poorly insulated walls, and creaking floors. But it had been built on a large piece of land with lots of maple trees. When June looked out her window, she could watch a farmer with his horse and plow

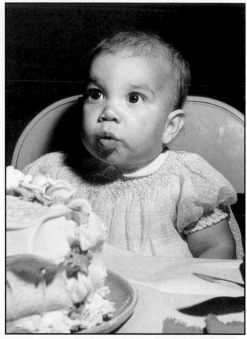

Above: The Fraynes, ca 1954

Above right: Jesse's first birthday

Right: June and Jesse, 1952

in a nearby field. It felt like living in the country. June and Trent have lived in that blue clapboard house ever since.

This is how June described the new comforts of her life in the 1950s:

After living through the Depression of the Thirties, during which almost all of us had known poverty's various humiliations, we were eating three times a day in houses with bay windows, a maple sapling in the front yard, and a car in the driveway. Our generation fought gallantly in the Second World War, Canadian infantry, sailors, and airmen always getting the dirtiest end of the stick. We had put our casualties and horrors behind us and were raising children who went to orthodontists.

Jill Frayne thought it was great fun growing up with two parents who were journalists:

My parents worked at home, their typewriters clacking away in the midst of family life, but they were always available to us. In the spring my father would cover baseball and the whole family would pack up and go to Florida for a month. We lived in a working-class neighborhood, where most families couldn't afford such a luxury. We were different. But in some ways I came from a typical family. I remember the Sunday drives out to Burlington for hot dogs.

Trent, June, and Trent's parents, Ella and Homer, with Casey

Jesse Frayne recalls their home life like this:

> For us, there was a great deal of stability because they both
> worked at home, though there were times we weren't sup-
> posed to disturb them and sometimes at dinner they'd still
> be mulling over their work. It was a Fifties family, with a very
> strong sense of work and of order.

Jesse adds that they weren't supposed to talk to their friends too much about going to Florida. They were encouraged not to think of themselves as special. However, Jesse desperately wanted a horse when she was six years old. Finally, when she was 12, she got her wish—a horse of her own to ride and care for.

June believes that children should be raised in some kind of religion, even if they reject it later

Jill, June, Brant, and Trent, 1949

Lady reporter interviews future King of Rock and Roll: June and Elvis Presley, 1957.

in life. The three children went to Sunday school at a nearby United Church, but Casey (their fourth child, born in 1962) refused to go. He was supposed to read the Bible instead, but he didn't. However, all the children grew up with a strong sense of what is right and wrong, and how to treat people fairly.

In the summers, the family sometimes drove to Port Dover, on Lake Erie. They ate hamburgers or hot dogs at the Arbour Restaurant, and then set up their towels and blankets a few feet from the water's edge. Later, they nibbled on fried perch from a sidewalk stand called Knetchel's, or walked along the pier to the lighthouse. They swam and relaxed all day. During those long summer days, June felt life was sweet.

June was developing a reputation as a fine journalist. Her colleagues came to admire and respect her. Robert Collins—teacher, journalist, editor, and author—once said, "And there was June Callwood, with the impossibly wholesome good looks of a Hollywood girl-next-door, who could write better than most of the men."

Robert Fulford, veteran journalist and broadcaster, culture critic, and award-winning editor, is another admirer of June's. He once declared, "June wrote with dash, flair, and originality. You could never predict what she was going to do. She knew how hard it was to write well."

One of June's favorite assignments was writing about Marilyn Bell, the teenage girl who was the first person to swim across Lake Ontario, in 1954. Marilyn was 16 years old, and the swim took almost 21 hours. June had only two days to write the article. She stayed up all night to finish it.

> The day that sixteen-year-old Marilyn Bell swam across Lake Ontario was a cold, sunny ninth of September. The small, tousle-haired Toronto schoolgirl swam forty miles from a log retaining wall in Youngstown, New York, to a slimy concrete breakwater off Sunnyside, Toronto's merry-go-round area, and thereby collected for herself whatever immortality awaits pioneer marathon swimmers, plus approximately $50,000 in contracts, prizes and gifts from Canadians who were moved by her courage.

During a dizzying five months in 1958, June wrote three different science articles for *Maclean's*. The first was about the universe ("What's Out There?"). The second was about the birth control pill ("How Good Is the Birth Control Pill?"). The third was about a special engine being built for a supersonic (faster than the speed of sound) Canadian airplane called the Avro Arrow ("The Day the Iroquois Flew"). Because of her love of flying, the scandalous story of the Arrow was one she would write and speak passionately about for years:

> It was the most beautiful plane I will ever see. Even parked on its stilt legs on the tarmac, it made your heart ache. When it lifted straight up into the sky, a slim white arrowhead, it was poetry. I never saw it take off without my eyes stinging, and I wasn't the only one.

The engine of the Avro Arrow, "the most beautiful plane I will ever see."

Briefly, here's the story. A team from the A.V. Roe Company in Malton (near Toronto) designed a state-of-the-art, supersonic jet for the Royal Canadian Air Force. They called it the Arrow.

In 1958, the prototype (test model) of the Arrow roared into the skies above Toronto on its first flight. During that year there were more than 50 test flights, using American engines. The engineers planned to develop a much more powerful Canadian engine, the PS-13 Iroquois, for the

June, third from left, with members of the U.S. Air Force, in Wichita, Kansas, 1947, on assignment for *Maclean's*

Arrow. The engine was supposed to be installed in March 1959. However, the Arrow was an expensive project, and the newly elected Conservative government, led by Prime Minister John Diefenbaker, decided to put an end to it.

On February 20, 1959, production of the Arrow and its Iroquois engine was halted dead in its tracks. That very day, more than 40,000 employees lost their jobs at Avro and its plants and suppliers. All designs, models, and blueprints were destroyed, and the planes were cut up with blowtorches. The Arrow turned into a $400-million pile of scrap metal, and many of the experts who had worked on it moved to the United States. Canada's aerospace industry has never recovered. That day in February has been called "Black Friday" ever since.

Elwy Yost—later a broadcaster, but then an employee of A.V. Roe—recalled how he felt when the Arrows were scrapped: "I will always remember the smell of the acetylene torches in the big hangars... The smell will live with me for the rest of my days. Seeing those beautiful planes being demolished—I'll never forgive them for that."

June was usually writing to a deadline. But how was she able to write so many articles on so many difficult topics in such a short space of time? And while taking care of a family besides? Her son, Brant, says that "she is extraordinarily intelligent, and a speed reader, as well as having a photographic memory." She often brought one or two children with her when she had to go to the office to write or revise an article. She worked on her story while a baby sat on her lap or a toddler played in a corner nearby. Jesse remembers playing under the typewriter table while her mother worked.

However, June set aside one day a week (Thursday) for interviewing people. On that day, she hired a babysitter named Dorothy Bland. She knew it would be too distracting to have a baby on her lap while she conducted interviews.

Furthermore, June has disciplined work habits. For example, when she's writing a book or magazine article, she usually works every day from eight in the morning until the middle of the afternoon. Sometimes she gets so caught up in her work that she loses track of what's going on around her. One time, she couldn't remember if she had given her children their lunch. Only the stack of dirty dishes in the sink proved that she had!

June is also very organized, and has an enormous amount of energy. When she decides something is important, she just does it.

In the 1950s, June had a doctor named Marion Hilliard, a well-known obstetrician who cared for many women in the writing community. The editor of *Chatelaine*, Gerry Anglin, admired Dr. Hilliard's strong views and wanted her to write for the magazine. However, Dr. Hilliard didn't have enough time to write an article on her own, so Gerry suggested she work with June. The collaboration suited Marion and June, and they went on to write several more articles. Then Doubleday, an American publisher, offered to put the articles together in a book. In 1957, *A Woman Doctor Looks at Life and Love* was published. The book became a bestseller and was eventually translated into 40 languages.

Soon afterwards, other opportunities came along for June to be a "ghostwriter." What is a ghostwriter? Suppose a publisher wants a famous person to write about his or her life, but maybe the celebrity is too busy, or doesn't have much talent for writing. The publisher then finds a writer who can help, but the story is told in the first person—"I, my"—as though the celebrity had written all of it. The actual writer remains as invisible as a ghost.

For many years, Doubleday used June as its regular ghostwriter. She interviewed the celebrity and other people, did further research, and wrote the book, but her name was seldom mentioned. She ghostwrote books for such people as television interviewer Barbara Walters (for Doubleday), and Canadian labor-union leader Bob White (for McClelland & Stewart). Robert Fulford said this about her ghostwriting: "Callwood has a special ability to get along with difficult and only slightly articulate people and translate their words into book-length manuscripts that sound as if they'd written them themselves."

Even if June didn't get her name on the books she ghostwrote, she had the satisfaction of knowing she had helped these important people tell their stories. Soon, though, she would become known for her own books.

By the late 1950s, with her three children in school, June began to suffer from depression—not just the sadness everybody feels at times, but a serious illness that can go on and on. When she found herself staring out the kitchen window for hours without noticing that time had passed, she realized that she needed help. She went to a therapist and gradually recovered. But her depression had drained away her happiness and energy for about a year—too much time.

Because June is an investigative journalist, she wanted to find out more about the condition she had suffered from. Her curiosity led her to do research about human emotions in general. It took five years, but her work resulted in the first book under her own name—*Love, Hate, Fear & Anger and Other Lively Emotions.* It was published in 1964 (and revised in 1986). This book was so good that it was used in many psychology courses at university. June knew how to explain a topic in a way that people could relate to and understand.

June herself would have liked to go to university, but in her earlier years there was never enough time or money. She had dreamed of becoming a lawyer like Grandfather Callwood, with a specialty in criminal law, or a doctor who did research. She would also have enjoyed the experience and learning that a university education would have given her. But even though she didn't have a university degree, she was writing books about difficult subjects—and she could choose subjects that had a personal meaning.

June Callwood was finding her voice. She was still a freelance journalist, writing "on demand," but she was beginning to discover the issues she cared deeply about. In the years ahead, she would use her writing skills—together with her passion—to defend the rights of countless people in need.

chapter 6
INTO THE FRAY:
DIGGER HOUSE (1968)

Yorkville, 1968

YORKVILLE IS NOW a fashionable shopping area, but in the early 1960s this corner of downtown Toronto was a neighborhood of rooming houses, musty bookstores, and coffee shops. Teenagers liked to go there to hear jazz or folk music in the bars or restaurants, to play chess, to smoke marijuana, and to hang out and talk about everything from philosophy to literature to politics. Yorkville had a certain romantic aura back then. It was *the* place to be, in what June once called "the sweet hippie time."

By the late 1960s, June and Trent's oldest three children had finished high school and young Casey was in school full time. Their older son, Barney, had left home and was living in Yorkville. By this time, Yorkville had changed dramatically. It wasn't romantic anymore. Once in a while, Barney met someone who needed help and he brought that young person back home. June and Trent gave the visitor something to eat and a place to sleep overnight.

June identified with these young people. She remembered the times when she was a teenager and her family was running from the sheriff because they couldn't pay the rent. She imagined that she herself could have turned into a troubled kid. Maybe she even wondered what might happen to Barney if he didn't have a home to come back to.

June was curious to see what Yorkville was really like by then, and how the area had been transformed during the decade. After all, she was an investigative journalist. So she went to find out.

"When I'd been there for a little while," she said, "I discovered that all those people who had talked about Kierkegaard and philosophy into the night had gone, and that the kids who were there were hungry and homeless. I stayed to see if I could help."

Many of the young people who lived around Yorkville had run away to Toronto from faraway places like Newfoundland or Saskatchewan, or even the United States. These "hippies" had dropped out of school and had few job skills. They had no place to take a shower or get clean clothes. They had to beg for food, and often went hungry. Some had no shoes. Some had bad teeth. Many were frequently victimized by drug dealers and pimps.

They couldn't get treatment in hospitals or receive welfare. Some ended up committing suicide, after losing confidence in themselves and hope for the future.

Few people in authority understood the hippies' problems. One city politician at the time even said, "Let them get cold and wet and dirty. It's not for the taxpayers to support them. Firemen should have the authority to hose them down, just like we hose down a street. The police should keep them on the move. The do-gooders don't know what the hell they're talking about."

June didn't let such words stop her. She remembered how it had been in Belle River, where people helped each other. She knew she had to do something for these young people. They desperately needed a safe place to live, where they could get decent food, medical treatment, and counseling. So June threw herself into creating a refuge for these street kids. She became an "activist," a person who actively works on social issues, instead of waiting for "the authorities" or "the system" to solve problems. She said, "I realized then that we had to change society. That radicalized me."

The result was Digger House—named after the Diggers, a group of people in England in the 1600s. They believed there was no place in society for the "ruling classes," and tried to create self-supporting communes.

How did it all happen? First, some young people got organized. They formed a corporation called Yorkville Diggers Inc., and went looking for funding. One of the leaders was David DePoe. He was a member of the Company of Young Canadians (CYC), a voluntary organization sponsored by the government of Canada. Brian (Blues) Chapman also got involved.

A former university student who had lived in Yorkville for years, he liked to wear an army surplus jacket stitched with embroidery. He helped kids when they had "bad trips" from drugs like LSD. According to June, artist Don Riggan was the most important youth leader of the Yorkville Diggers, because he stayed with June during the whole process of getting the house started, while David and Brian moved on to other things.

June speaks at a fundraising event.

The young leaders had no knowledge of City Hall's rules and regulations about such homes, and no experience with permits and inspectors. David DePoe once said, "It must really be a drag to work in City Hall. Let's come down one day and give flowers to them all." But the organizers knew they'd have to get money, and then find a building that would suit their purposes. Little did they guess how difficult the undertaking would be.

June asked religious organizations for money, and a group of seven churches and synagogues donated funds to support the home for a "lengthy period" of time. United, Presbyterian, Catholic, Anglican, and Unitarian churches pitched in, as did Holy Blossom Temple and Beth Tzedec Synagogue. A letter from this interfaith group explained, "We were impressed by the humanitarian aspects of the venture and the promise it holds of relieving some of the problems in Yorkville which concern us deeply."

The Yorkville Diggers also obtained money from the Alcoholism and Drug Addiction Foundation as well as the government of Metropolitan Toronto. The most significant source of funding was a three-year grant of $81,000 from the federal Department of Health and Welfare.

Even after the money was raised, it was an uphill battle to find a suitable building. From early spring of 1967 until the winter of 1968, June and the organizing committee kept looking for a house. But a lot of landlords were suspicious of the hippies and refused to rent a property to them. They thought the residents would be noisy, dirty, and worst of all, high on drugs. One prospect after another fell through.

Finally, in January 1968, the city itself supplied the answer. The Diggers could rent a 14-room house at 115 Spadina Road, which was slated for demolition and was owned by the city. The organizers knew they couldn't afford to buy a building, so renting one would have to do for the time being. They were desperate to find a shelter for the young people living on the streets or in condemned buildings during the depths of winter.

June had been appealing to various organizations to cover the rent and operating expenses. But before any money came through, the house became available. So June paid the first month's rent out of her own pocket. As she said years later, "I decided I was a church, too." In addition, she and psychiatrist Dr. John Rich had to sign the lease. Two Diggers had intended to sign it, but the city wanted "reputable citizens" to be responsible. And they wouldn't let a woman sign a lease alone.

The house was in terrible shape. Only the first and second floors were ever used, because the third floor was unsafe. To make the house livable, the City of Toronto paid $556 for electrical repairs and the Diggers paid $400 for carpentry. About $400 for plumbing was donated. Other work needed doing—then and later—but Digger House always suffered from a lack of money.

Digger House in 1969

In February 1968, Digger House finally opened its doors, and quickly became a relief center for dropouts, runaways, and kids in trouble with drugs. On the first night, over 100 kids "crashed" there. The fire department intervened after that and capped the residency at 20. June's son Brant volunteered to take charge of the head count until Digger House could afford to hire staff. He said, "The kids who come here are trying to do something positive with their lives and we're trying to help them." Brant also explained, "Like, I don't lay down rules and regulations and that kind of stuff. I guess you can say my role is to remember what other people forget." But there were rules, all the same: no liquor, no disorderly behavior, and no drugs or sex on the premises. However, there was no set rule about how long someone could stay. The young people drifted in and out. By the summer of 1968, trouble was brewing.

June's growing activism soon led her into conflict with the authorities. On the evening of July 10, 1968, she joined a demonstration by a group of young people. They were protesting the two-year jail sentence given in Boston to Dr. Benjamin Spock, the famous American pediatrician for "conspiracy to aid, abet, and counsel young men to avoid the draft."

Four young protesters sat down in the middle of Yorkville Avenue, bringing traffic to a halt. Other protesters surged onto the road, until the police arrived to break up the demonstration.

A police officer took one of the protesters down an alley to a waiting police car, and June was worried the youth would get beaten up. In those days the police were very suspicious of the hippies, with their long hair, bare feet, and lack of respect for authority. Officers were poorly trained to deal with hippies in Yorkville, and consequently often used more force than they should have.

June followed the young man and the officer. The officer ordered her to leave, insisting that it wasn't her business. June retorted, "Yes it is. I'm responsible for him and you're responsible to me and we're both responsible to each other."

She was promptly arrested, put in a police wagon, and taken off to Toronto's Don Jail. As the police wagon pulled away, a crowd of about 450 people jeered and pelted it with soft-drink cans and garbage. June was later charged with obstructing police.

This was a minor charge, but June was devastated. Here she was, a well-known writer, the wife of a prominent journalist, and the mother of four, thrown into a dark and smelly jail cell. The walls, bench, and toilet had been smeared with shit. She felt humiliated and angry. She was worried that no one would ever talk to her or hire her again. She did a lot of crying in the jail cell that night. She later said, "In my generation, you didn't get arrested unless you were an awful person."

Fortunately, things didn't turn out as badly as she had feared. She was released on bail early the next morning. Pierre Berton himself testified at her trial, more than three months later. She was promptly acquitted, but the judge advised her to be more "prudent" if she went back to Yorkville. Prudent? Not likely. The experience had shown June the importance of being an advocate, speaking up for people living on the edge.

Getting arrested was one of the events that turned June into an activist. It is her firm belief that in life "there are no innocent bystanders." In the village of Belle River, everyone had helped everyone else. She wanted people in the big city to feel involved and responsible, too.

The evening after her night in jail, June attended a cocktail party at the home of Frank Shuster. Shuster and his partner, Johnny Wayne, were TV stars—the famous Wayne and Shuster comedy team—and this party was for the "crème de la crème" of Toronto's society. June told the other guests about Digger House, about the "hell of the lost kids" who went there "out of a nightmare of nowheres." People wrote checks and pledged money.

June intervened when police led a young protester away. She was arrested shortly thereafter.

In 1969, B'nai B'rith Women, now called Jewish Women International of Canada (JWIC), gave June their award for "Woman of the Year." JWIC is an organization that works to end violence against women. It values a society where "women live in a spirit of tolerance, safety, and security." The award came at just the right time, for June was still feeling downhearted about having been arrested.

Over the next few years, the organizers of Digger House tried to get more funding, but they ultimately failed. Why did this happen? One reason was that many older people in authority were suspicious about, or downright antagonistic to, these young people who needed help. A man from the Council on Drug Abuse wrote, "We are all very much averse to using public funds to promote and encourage aimless, pleasure-seeking living..."

In February 1972, funding ran out and Digger House was forced to close. During its existence, the refuge had sheltered over a thousand homeless young people—no mean feat for a house that grew out of an idea and a few people's determination.

June later called Digger House a "Band-Aid solution," meaning it only offered temporary help, not a permanent improvement. June had been hoping to change the system that had caused the problems in the first place. However, she learned some important lessons from the experience—about herself as well as about government bureaucracy. "I seem to guilt myself a lot less if I interfere when something isn't fair—even if I screw up the intervention, even if it doesn't succeed—than if I decide injustice isn't my business and pass by."

Incidentally, in the 1970s June undertook a one-woman letter-writing campaign to close the oldest section of the Don Jail. Her one night there had affected her so strongly that she didn't want anyone else to go through the same degrading experience. June wrote to everyone from the prime minister to the health department. She focused on the fact that the jail provided less space for its inmates than the San Diego Zoo gave its orangutans. The activism worked, and in late 1977 it was June who swung the gold-painted mallet to begin the demolition of the cramped, outdated building.

June had stepped out of the warmth and comfort of her own home to help create a refuge for others. Instead of walking by and looking the other way, as so many people did, she had joined hands with those who needed help, and had added her voice—her strong, clear voice—to their pleas. And she would do it again.

The Spadina Road residence that once was Digger House, as it is today

chapter 7
FINDING SHELTER: NELLIE'S (1974)

AROUND THE TIME WHEN Yorkville Digger House had to shut down, the nearby YWCA shelter for women also closed. June became concerned about homeless teenage women. Vicki Trerise, who had run the YWCA shelter, was also worried about the problem. A number of other women joined them and began work to create a new shelter. Eventually, they named it "Nellie's."

Almost from the beginning, Nellie's was based on a cooperative, egalitarian model. The board of directors was made up of volunteers, but the staff doing the day-to-day work attended all meetings of the board and its committees. Decisions about fundraising and running the organization were made by everyone, by achieving consensus (mutual agreement), so formal votes were never needed.

At first, the board members had two priorities: to raise money and to locate a suitable building. It took time, but finally they found a handsome Victorian-style house on Broadview Avenue. Nellie's opened its doors in June 1974.

At the time Nellie's was founded, the feminist movement was becoming a strong force. Feminists believe that a woman's role—her work, her

Early Canadian feminist Nellie McClung, whose legacy was honored in the naming of Nellie's.

An eight cent Canadian postage stamp was also issued in honor of Nellie in 1973.

rights, and her freedom—should never be limited by the fact that she is female.

June didn't become a feminist until the early 1970s, when something "clicked." Feminism gradually "sneaked up" on her, she says, as she wrote about issues like abortion, day-care centers, and the scarcity of women in politics. She came to the conclusion that women and men sometimes perceive things differently; that both their views are valuable and need to be considered. "Women have different ears. Maybe not better, but they hear different things." But she also believes that feminism is about getting equality not only for women but for men, too. She points out that "there's no improvement in the human condition in replacing discrimination against women with discrimination against men."

The women, young or old, who came to the hostel were desperate for help. In the beginning, most of them were homeless. Some had psychiatric or addiction problems. Nellie's tried to take them all in, but because of fire regulations, not more than 30 women were allowed to stay at one time. Almost every night, the staff had to turn women away. However, first they would phone other hostels to see if there was room somewhere else.

Nellie's is a huge house with bedrooms on three floors. The program manager at Nellie's describes it like this: "Nellie's has a home-like atmosphere. There are drapes in the windows, a living room, dining room, free access to the kitchen. It's not a home, but we try to make it feel like one."

Residents are allowed to stay a maximum of three weeks (four if they have children with them). They have a safe place to sleep and nutritious food to eat. They have time to decide what to do next with their lives. Meanwhile, Nellie's staff members work with agencies around Toronto to find long-term, low-cost housing for these women.

All the board members, including June, did their share to support the staff. For example, they took turns cooking Sunday dinners for the residents in order to give the staff a break. Sometimes June even worked a 16-hour night shift. She answered the phone, accepted women who came to the door if there was room, or chatted with women who couldn't sleep.

The years passed, and June became involved with other groups that helped people in need. Some of these were human-rights organizations such as the

Canadian Civil Liberties Association, the Canadian Council of Christians and Jews, and PEN Canada, an organization that defends writers persecuted for expressing their opinions.

She went back to writing on a regular basis for the *Globe and Mail*. From 1975 to 1978 she did in-depth profiles about women titled "The informal..." She later wrote a column from 1983 to 1989 in which she focused on people and social issues such as family violence, day-care centers, human rights, prisons, and censorship. She was also busy writing books. She wrote two books about women and the law with Marvin Zuker, a lawyer and educator; a book about Canadian history called *Portrait of Canada*; and others. As always, the books reflected her passionate commitment to social justice.

Meanwhile at Nellie's, staff person Diane Capponi had written a proposal to establish a drop-in resource center. It would be a place where women who were not residents could talk to staff members while their children were in a day-care center. The women would also be able to attend nutrition classes, speak to a nurse, get advice about work or personal matters, or even improve their reading and writing skills.

In 1991, staff and some board members asked June to come back on the board and help get this project off the ground since funding was hard to obtain. June and Diane met with a provincial civil servant, and work was begun on a fundraising concert called "On Stage for Nellie's."

At a December meeting in a basement room at Nellie's, with staff and board members sitting in a circle, June announced that she had found some funding for the project. But then a Black female staff member raised another issue. She complained that the white staff was being racist. June challenged her on this, and tempers flared. In the heat of the ensuing argument, someone called June a racist.

June was stunned. She took off her glasses, gathered up her papers, and left the room. Out in the hallway, she was so upset that she had to stop and pull herself together before she could drive home.

Others there leapt to her defense, including those few who knew how hard June had worked to protect another Black woman, when that woman had been threatened with deportation. Eventually the accusation of racism was withdrawn, but damage had been done. To this day the whole blow-up remains a painful memory for her. "I was in bad shape for a long time," June says. "It took me years to stop being angry, and I'm not over being hurt yet."

Months passed. In April 1992 June went through with plans for "On Stage for Nellie's." The event raised more than $22,000. Shortly afterwards, June resigned from Nellie's board of directors. One journalist said, "June Callwood's replacement at Nellie's will have a very hard time outpacing her generosity and wisdom in the social-service arena."

After June left, things at Nellie's went from bad to worse. Staff and board members were in continual conflict. Staff members made more demands and filed more complaints. Twelve members of the board had resigned by November 1992.

In 1995, some of the money raised at a dinner in June's honor was given to Nellie's—quietly and without fanfare. Nellie's has since expanded to include support in the community after residents leave the shelter. The vision of a drop-in resource center has become a reality. However, the rift between June and Nellie's has never healed.

Nellie's has helped over 25,000 women and children since it was founded back in 1974. Of course, it would be ideal if a shelter like Nellie's were no longer needed. "But as long as there is abuse," said one board member when Nellie's celebrated its twenty-fifth anniversary in 1999, "as long as there is homelessness, there will always be a Nellie's."

chapter 8
CHILDREN RAISING CHILDREN: JESSIE'S CENTRE (1982)

THE 1980S WERE DIFFICULT YEARS for June and her family. The decade began with a terrible accident.

In November 1980, June's daughter Jill, who was 35 years old, was riding her bicycle in downtown Toronto. The driver of a cement truck didn't see her, and as he turned the corner he ran her over. Jill was dragged under the truck for a distance and suffered grave injuries. Her doctors thought she might not live. Even if she survived, they said, she would never walk again.

The family was devastated by Jill's accident, but everyone pulled together. Trent helped Jill feel better with his special kind of humor and caring attention. Although Brant and Jesse weren't living at home anymore, they did everything they could for their sister. Casey was in his first year at Queen's University, but he treated Jill with gentle kindness when he came home to visit at Christmas.

June spent long hours every day in the hospital with Jill. After Jill came home, June took care of her while she recuperated for a few months. She created a cocoon of peace and quiet for her daughter; she cooked Jill's favorite foods and brought her cups of tea. After a long year of suffering and recovery, Jill proved the doctors wrong. She did walk again, eventually without a cane. As for the truck driver, he was fined $100 for making an unsafe turn.

June didn't let her personal worries stop her from working on an important project she had already begun. In the 1970s, if you were a pregnant unmarried teenager, you had limited choices—have an abortion, get married, or give up your baby for adoption. In those days, about one-quarter of single pregnant teenagers had abortions; most of the rest chose adoption. It wasn't a simple matter to get an abortion. Starting in 1969, abortion was allowed in Canada only if the mother's health was in danger; not until 1988 could a woman get an abortion because she believed it was the best thing to do.

By the 1980s, a fourth option was becoming more widespread—about 85 percent of unwed teen mothers were keeping their babies. But they faced a lot of challenges, for there were no support services to help them. Many of the mothers were quite young. Most were poor, and many had dropped out of school and didn't have job skills. How could these "children raising children" cope with the demands of parenthood? Very often, their babies were at risk because the mothers didn't know how to keep an infant healthy and safe. They didn't know about formula and baby vitamins, or about colic and diaper rash and other infant medical problems. They didn't know what to do when the baby cried or fussed or wouldn't sleep. Sometimes, if the mothers felt lonely and helpless, they made dangerous lifestyle choices that put themselves and their babies at even more risk, like leaving their babies alone or with an incompetent caregiver.

Late in 1979, June got to know a group of women who were meeting regularly in a basement room at Nellie's Hostel. They wanted to create a centrally located place that would offer a complete package of support—group and individual counseling, a nursery, used clothes and toys, a medical clinic, help in finding housing, and even teachers, so the teens could continue their education.

When June came on the scene, she helped pull the project together. She chaired the committee of women and did much of the fundraising. Her enthusiasm for this project came partly from her sympathy for the mothers, and partly from her belief that "If you do certain things to a baby for 18 months, you can definitely produce a rather resilient human being with a sense of self-worth. If we would just do this... for one generation, we could change the world."

June found a two-storey former car-repair shop on Bathurst Street, in downtown Toronto, that would be used for the drop-in center. They called the center after June's younger daughter, Jesse (with a different spelling), because it seemed like a warm, friendly name. They sealed up the garage door, put down carpet, installed new plumbing and lighting, and redecorated. On the main floor there was a lounge, kitchen, diaper-changing area, baby-bathing area, and nursery. Upstairs there was space for classes and counseling sessions. In January 1982, Jessie's Centre for Teenagers finally opened its doors.

Many pregnant teens who come to Jessie's are looking for advice. Should they keep their babies or make another choice? One young mother described the loneliness of her pregnancy, and the importance of Jessie's:

June inside Jessie's Centre

"At first, I felt I was the only one it was happening to. The pregnancy felt like a disease. I wanted to hide. Young friends all drift away because of your new responsibilities… I found new friends at Jessie's. I didn't feel so left out anymore."

Another young mother explained that "when you come to Jessie's, you have all the options in one space and no one is going to say, 'You're stupid for getting pregnant.' They leave the choice up to you and then help you with whatever choice you make… They're not judging you as a *kid* with a baby. They're looking at you as a *person* with a baby."

Jessie's was soon too small to serve all the young women who were asking for help. Peter Bronfman, a businessman who was involved in many charities, helped raise $1.8 million to fund a bigger and better building. Jack Diamond, a well-known architect, designed a beautiful, light-filled six-storey building, including four floors of apartments for low-income families. In 1991, Jessie's moved to its new home at Queen and Parliament Streets, in the east end of Toronto.

Even though there are now many ways to prevent unwanted pregnancy, Jessie's Centre for Teenagers is still a vitally needed service. In 2003, about 33,000 women aged 15 to 19 became pregnant in Canada. About 15,000 of them gave birth. Many of them did not have the knowledge and support they needed to care for their infants. Jessie's still helps about 500 teenage families every year.

When you enter Jessie's, you see strollers and infant car seats clustered near the front door. Colorful posters and a painted rainbow decorate the pale yellow walls. While babies and toddlers are cared for in the nursery, which has gorgeous stained-glass windows, some of the young mothers study with a teacher. They concentrate on English, math, and computer skills. Some are trying to finish high school; others are learning skills like cooking and child care.

Inside Jessie's

The stained glass window by Sarah Hall is a favorite of the kids at Jessie's.

June with a young Jessie's Centre client

Some of the young men and women who are a part of Jessie's

The young mothers can also attend sessions about health care. They can pick up emergency supplies of baby formula and diapers, and go to the "swap shop" to get maternity clothes and baby clothes. There's even a full-time nurse on staff, and a doctor who comes in once a week to run a free medical clinic.

When people worry about young mothers and their babies, sometimes the teenage dads are overlooked. But at Jessie's there is a special program for them. The young men learn how to make formula, change diapers, and cuddle their babies. One father said, "This is the first place I've ever been where people pay attention to *me*."

When the young women move on as confident mothers who have found their place in the world, they don't forget the help they received. As one of Jessie's ex-clients says:

I often think about how much Jessie's has helped my daughter Hailey and me make it through the struggles and get to a place of comfort and security in our lives. When people find out I had Hailey so young, they often ask me, "How did you do it?"—and my reply always mentions the support of Jessie's, and my family and friends.

Jessie's Centre

chapter 9
REMEMBERING CASEY: CASEY HOUSE (1988)

IN APRIL OF 1982, a few months after Jessie's Centre opened, Casey Frayne came home for a visit after writing his exams for third-year engineering at Queen's University, in Kingston. He had supper with his parents at the Peter Pan restaurant, hugged them goodbye, got on his motorcycle, and started out on the three-hour ride back to Kingston.

Trent, June, and Casey in Italy, 1972

Casey never got there. The driver of an oncoming car veered into his lane and crashed head-on into his motorcycle. Casey Frayne died a few hours later, in Oshawa General Hospital. He was only 20 years old.

The sorrow of losing her youngest child is something June has never fully recovered from. She says, "The death of a child is the worst experience there is in life." Their friends rallied around the family, but there was little they could say or do. As Pierre Berton described it, "When we hugged his parents at the funeral, it was as if we were hugging one of our own, knowing, at the same time, that no gestures from us could relieve the torture they were going through." Trent and June didn't leave each other's side for the next two weeks.

They went to Kingston to collect Casey's belongings from the house he had shared with three other students. Because he had just written his

In the garden where Casey's ashes are buried

final exams, Casey hadn't had time to do his laundry. June gathered up his dirty jeans, shirts, underwear, and socks from the hamper. She brought them home, washed and ironed them, and put them away in his room. She knew it didn't make sense—none of it made sense—but it was something she had to do.

After Casey was cremated, they buried his ashes under the apple tree in the side yard where he had played as a child. The tree is just outside June's office window.

Though many people thought the driver who killed Casey was drunk, she was convicted of a much less serious offense—careless driving. As a result, she got only a three-month suspension of her license and a $500 fine. (Even if she had been convicted of impaired driving, the penalty would have been minor. In those days, impaired driving wasn't considered a serious offence. Since 2000, the maximum penalty for impaired driving causing death has been life imprisonment.)

A heartbroken June said, "Whatever the punishment, Casey will not walk through our door again." Nothing would bring back their shy, cheerful son, the brother Jill Frayne called "the sweetest person on earth." Only after his death did they find out that Casey had been a regular blood donor, and had also given all of his prize money from school awards to the Canadian Cancer Society in honor of a friend who had died of brain cancer. Casey had refused to go to Sunday school, but he had known how to be a kind and generous person.

In her grief, June threw herself even more tirelessly into her work. In the spring of 1985, she was involved with a group of about 60 people who had banded together to help Margaret Frazer, a retired high-school teacher who was dying of cancer. Margaret wanted to stay in her own home, surrounded by cherished objects she had collected during her life. She wanted to listen to her music, walk in her garden, and pet her cat, Cleo.

Margaret's friends and acquaintances, soon to be called the "Margaret Team," provided round-the-clock care and support. They fed her, brushed her hair, helped her get dressed, and did all kinds of other tasks—many of them messy and even unpleasant. They worked together to help Margaret cope with her pain and loneliness for twelve long weeks. She passed away in her home, as she had wanted to.

After Margaret died, June wrote a book describing how all these people had worked together, in spite of their own conflicted feelings about illness and death. She wrote that a crisis like someone else's death releases our "better being," for "people respond in a time of peril with a strength they never knew before and are grateful to find that splendid self within." And she noted that the helpers themselves benefit from helping others. "For the individual who experiences it, it has the distinct feeling of growth; for the human tribe, it is a redemptive experience."

June's book, *Twelve Weeks in Spring*, was published in 1986. It became a bestseller. The experience of helping Margaret Frazer die in her own home made June think about the fact that hospitals tend to treat death like a medical problem, rather than the final stage of life. Also, most hospitals are noisy, sterile, lonely institutions. As June says in *Twelve Weeks in Spring*, "Hospitals were never intended to be places where people go to die. The primary function of hospital care is to heal." But around this same time, there was a special need for places where dying people could find refuge.

In the early 1980s, there was a lot of fear and ignorance about HIV (Human Immunodeficiency Virus), which usually results in AIDS (Acquired Immune Deficiency Syndrome). At first, people thought AIDS was a disease that infected only gay men, people who injected drugs and shared needles, and people with hemophilia. (Hemophilia leads to uncontrolled bleeding, so people with this disorder often need blood transfusions. In those early days, some people caught AIDS from infected transfusions.) At that time, many people didn't realize that a person could be infected with HIV and not show symptoms for years, or that seemingly healthy women and children could be infected, too. AIDS didn't even have a name until 1982.

This strange new infection created a lot of fear and suspicion. Sometimes those who had the disease were fired from their jobs, or were refused housing. They were often isolated from their friends and families because of the shame surrounding the disease. Many were left to die a lonely death in the hospital, for as one doctor said, "People with AIDS are this century's lepers. No one wants to touch them." Even health-care workers didn't understand how HIV was transmitted. They entered the hospital room fully gowned and gloved, and left food trays outside the patient's door.

June wanted to use half the royalties from *Twelve Weeks in Spring* to fund a cause that reflected what the Margaret Team had learned about palliative care. Because conditions for people dying of AIDS were so appalling, June approached ACT (the AIDS Committee of Toronto) in the mid-1980s to ask if it was planning an AIDS hospice and if she could help. ACT told June that it was too busy creating buddy programs and support for people with AIDS, but would be happy if she wanted to try to establish a hospice. ACT offered her meeting space in its office and use of its tax registration number.

What is a hospice? It's a place where someone with an incurable disease can die with a minimum of pain in a comfortable, home-like, friendly environment. In a hospice especially for people with AIDS, everyone would understand the problem and be sympathetic. The staff would be experts on AIDS, instead of fearing it as if it were a dreadful mystery. People suffering from the disease could comfort and support each other. Their families and partners could also get the support they needed.

Even today, hospices are not yet widespread, especially in North America. Although some hospitals have "palliative-care" sections where people are cared for in the final stages of an incurable disease, a hospital is still, generally, not a good place to die. June believes that "dying is very much like being born. Dying people need to be held, to be soothed, to be sung to, to be rocked. It's quite clear to me that the circle comes around. If you nurture them as you would a baby, you've got it right."

In September 1985, the first meeting to create a Toronto AIDS hospice took place. About 30 people gathered together in the ACT offices, above a Kentucky Fried Chicken store. June had invited people from the government to "make sure we got it right." She had been spreading the word about the hospice, and that everyone was welcome to come to the meeting. There were representatives from ACT, doctors and nurses active in the small AIDS community, and former members of the Margaret Team from Holy Trinity Anglican Church and Nellie's, among others.

The organizing group called itself the "ACT Steering Committee for AIDS Hospice." They established the three principles for a hospice, all of equal importance: top-of-the-line medical expertise, along with complementary therapies, such as massage and acupuncture; a team-like environment among staff and volunteers; and respect for the dying person's wishes.

At that first meeting June struck three sub-committees and asked people to chair them. They were to find a building, to raise money, and to design the program (since there was no existing AIDS hospice to use as a model). Now they could begin.

The plan was to establish a hospice that was separate from any hospital. The goal was to raise $750,000 (about half the amount that was eventually needed). The group did a lot of work seeking funds from individuals, government, businesses, and charitable foundations. As she had planned, June donated half of her royalties from *Twelve Weeks in Spring* to the cause.

The volunteers found a 30-room Victorian house on Huntley and Isabella Streets, in the heart of the gay neighborhood in downtown Toronto. The house had been used as a bed-and-breakfast and was in very good condition. However, it took a lot of hard work to turn it into a modern healthcare facility: wiring and plumbing had to be changed, walls had to be moved, and a nursing station had to be built. The cost of the renovation was $800,000, even though many of the furnishings, all of the art, and some of the construction was donated. Volunteer painters, carpenters, and decorators gave their time and skill to get the place ready for the people who so desperately needed a hospice.

On March 1, 1988, Casey House—named in memory of Casey Frayne, who had died so young—officially opened. It was the world's first hospice for people with AIDS. Its motto was "Give Compassion a Home."

One person who needed Casey House was Jim St. James. June had met Jim, a former actor, in late summer 1986. Although he had suffered for years with AIDS, he was a spokesperson for others with the disease and a founding member of the Toronto PWA (People with AIDS) Coalition. He helped people with AIDS get together and support each other.

June wrote a book about Jim and Casey House, called *Jim: A Life with AIDS*. She described how people reacted to the AIDS crisis in the autumn of 1987:

> As in a garrison under siege from a merciless enemy, gay people tended one another. Nobility emerged as people turned their minds to living each day as if it were their last. Stories of extraordinary kindness abounded, and expressions of affection were less restrained. A gentleness settled on the community; its suffering brought with it dignity and strength.

June's book helped people understand the suffering of people with AIDS, and the importance of sanctuaries like Casey House. She wrote that Jim St. James "told friends he had never known such calm and peace in his whole life. Living for four years with a fatal disease had not instilled in him any fear of death; instead he had developed an intense appreciation of life." When Jim died at Casey House in 1990, June and another friend, Theresa Dobko from ACT, were at his side.

Casey House

When you enter Casey House, the first thing that strikes you is that it looks like someone's lovely home, and not like a hospital. Everything is calm and orderly. The walls are painted a muted shade of rose. Beautiful pieces of art by well-known Canadian artists such as Joyce Wieland and Ronald Bloore hang in various rooms.

On the first floor are the reception area, several lounges with comfortable chairs, a massage-therapy room, and a few residents' rooms. There's also a Quiet Room, with stained-glass windows of birds and flowers, where people can go to think or talk or pray. There are more residents' rooms on the second floor. Residents can bring personal items such as photos, rocking chairs, aquariums, and stuffed toys, so they'll feel more at home. Each room has a computerized bed that can shift the person's position automatically, as well as a television and CD player. There's also a special bathtub that's big enough to hold someone on a stretcher.

There are always people waiting for a place in Casey House. Since it opened, about 3,000 people have been cared for—men, women, and even children. All the patients have HIV/AIDS, and some have been turned away by their families and have felt rejected by society. One of the nurses says, "They are being fully accepted for the first time in their lives... We must be doing something right. Casey House works."

You might think it's a sad place, and in a way it is. But it's also a home where people care for each other like a family, giving each other lots of hugs, and showing their concern for each other day by day and hour by hour. It's a place where people can die with as little distress as possible, or extend their lives and go home again. And it's not just the residents who get treatment. Through its home hospice service, Casey House cares for about 120 non-residents every day, with nursing, physiotherapy, social work, and nutrition counseling.

After the death of a resident, or someone in the home-care program, or a close friend of Casey House, a candle is lit and placed on a beautiful desk by the front window, to burn for 24 hours. June says, "Neighbors who pass by tell me that they offer a prayer when they see the candle is lit." Relatives and friends often write in the Remembrance Book that is kept on the desk beside the candle. One person wrote, "To Casey House and its staff: I was and still am overwhelmed by your amazing love." And every year, volunteers make a quilt with the names of the people who have died during the past year. The quilt hangs in a place of honor in the main lounge, while quilts of past years are rolled up and stored away with love and respect.

The people at Casey House like to tell this story. Before the house was purchased, graphics designer, Bernie Stockl, donated the Casey House logo to June and the organizing group. He created an open door with a heart in it. During the renovations months later, the organizers ended a meeting and were leaving through the side door, which faces west. Looking up as the setting sun shone through a stained-glass window above the door, the group saw for the first time that the window contained a red heart. It was exactly the image the group had chosen for its logo.

That's what Casey House is—an open door, and a heart.

June with grandson Jack Manchester, 10, at the Pride Parade, 1998

chapter 10
A LIFE WELL LIVED

IN 1992, JUNE'S DAUGHTER JILL gave her a unique birthday present—an introductory flight on a glider plane at the Beaver Valley Soaring Club near Collingwood, Ontario. June had never flown a glider before, but she loved being back up in the air.

It took her three sum-mers to get her glider-pilot license, but gliding became one of her favorite activities. And although she was over 70, she wasn't content to glide lazily above the clouds and coast gently back down to earth—not June! She loved to do aerobatics, like flying in loops. She felt free as a bird catching the warm currents of air above Georgian Bay, float-ing close to nature. She calls

Celebrating her first solo flight

Turning 60 in style

it "being on the edge of bliss."

June also loves to swim three times a week. To her, swimming feels almost like flying; both have a spiritual quality. One of her pleasures is to go somewhere warm—maybe Florida or an island in the Caribbean—and take along plenty of books, trail mix, and fruit. Then she reads and swims all day long. She may also watch the people, or the birds flying overhead. Closing her eyes for long periods of time, she feels the surf "unknotting my soul." After such a short holiday, she is ready to face the world again.

June and Trent's grown-up children have had their own successes and challenges. Years after her accident, Jill wrote a book called *Starting Out in the Afternoon: A Mid-Life Journey into Wild Land*. It tells the story of her three-month trip to British Columbia, where she went sea kayaking, discovered the wilderness, and learned what is important to her in life. The book was nominated for a Governor General's Award in 2002.

Jill now lives north of Algonquin Park, in Ontario, and works part-time as a family therapist in a mental-health center. Her daughter, Bree, lives in New York City and often comes to Toronto to visit the family. Bree's name is still on the door of one of the bedrooms in the blue clapboard house that June and Trent bought so many years ago.

In her book, Jill wrote, "My mother and father taught all four of us to love words and to find comfort in writing. Their influence is the slow-acting wave, the one that started long ago and has been gathering all my life. They still set the standard in every way I can think of."

June and Trent's son Brant was the host of a television show on the CBC for two seasons and wanted to become a film producer. But in 1993 doctors discovered that Brant had an aneurysm (a bubble in an artery) in his brain, and he had to have emergency surgery. During the operation, his brain didn't get enough oxygen, and Brant had a stroke. He became paralyzed on the left side of his body.

Brant tried with all his might to get better, but the paralysis has never gone away. In 2003 he published an article about his experiences, called "My First Death," in *Toronto Life* magazine. "My mother had already lost one son, and I wasn't sure she could bear to lose another," he wrote. The article won the silver prize for "Personal Journalism" in the National Magazine Awards.

June with her grandchildren, Lucy and Jack Manchester

Three generations: Daughters Jill and Jesse, grandchildren Emma and Marie Manchester and Bree Fitzgerald

Brant has a small apartment in Toronto, and is trying his best to live his life with his disability. As he said in his article, "The old Brant is a neat suit of clothes hanging in a closet; the new me is a mess of thread and fabric remnants and a complicated sewing machine I hope one day I will learn to manage using one hand." Despite the challenges he faces, Brant follows his mother's example of helping others. He has been supporting a foster child, a boy in Sri Lanka, for years.

June and Trent's younger daughter, Jesse, lives in Toronto with her husband, Mark. They have four children. In 2002, Jesse wrote a popular cookbook called *Great Food for Happy Kids*. She also wrote a mystery novel called *Just Keep Breathing* that was published in the fall of 2005. It would seem that June and Trent passed on a "writing gene" to their children.

Even though Casey Frayne was killed at such a young age, he left a lasting legacy. Because of Casey's death, John Bates, the father of one of Casey's friends at Burnhamthorpe Collegiate, became one of the founders of an organization called Mothers Against Drunk Driving (MADD). This group of citizens has worked to bring about laws to stop impaired driving and to support victims of this crime. Andrew Murie of MADD Canada says, "Impaired driving remains, by far, the single largest criminal cause of death in Canada. Even conservatively estimated, alcohol and/or drug-impaired driving in Canada resulted in over 1,250 deaths and 74,000 injuries in 2003."

Partners for life

After more than 60 years of marriage, June and Trent are still close and loving. They still make each other laugh and their affection shows in everything they do. For example, Trent gets up early in the morning to read the sports pages and eat a quiet breakfast by himself in the kitchen. Then he prepares fruit, toast, and herbal tea for June, and she eats her breakfast while reading the Toronto newspapers or *The New York Times*.

Trent has always wanted June to do whatever she found fulfilling. When an interviewer asked what the secret of their marriage was, June answered, "I live with a man who is very honest and very kind. He is just not a man who seems to be threatened, so it doesn't ask very much to live with him." What they both know is how to respect each other's differences. June isn't interested in sports; Trent doesn't get involved in June's causes; and that's fine with both of them.

The old house in Toronto is still the place where June and Trent, their three children and five grandchildren, and assorted other relatives and friends gather for birthdays or Christmas or Thanksgiving. When the family is all sitting around the table, June feels truly happy.

June with Marie and Emma Manchester

June works in a small study off the dining room; she likes to be in the middle of the action. Her desk sits beneath a window where she can look out at the garden, and at Casey's apple tree. Light streams in and illuminates family photos, certificates, and works of art that hang on the wall.

When she's not busy in her office, June likes to drive around Toronto in her dark brown Mazda sports car. She may visit the mothers and babies at Jessie's Centre or help out at Casey House. While driving, she listens to singers like Chet Baker and Johnny Cash. She also loves music by Bach, Vivaldi, and Beethoven, as well as arias from Verdi operas. Music soothes her soul.

June's main cause nowadays is to eliminate child poverty. She is deeply concerned that over a million children in Canada (nearly one in six) live in poverty. She is co-chair of the Campaign Against Child Poverty (CACP), along with Arthur Bielfeld, Rabbi Emeritus of Temple Emanu-El in Toronto. The CACP is made up of citizens from all across Canada—from different religions, charities, and child-welfare organizations. One of their aims is to get more funding from government for child-care centers, as well as better salaries for child-care workers.

June Callwood is over 80 years old now. How does she find the energy for all her causes? One friend explains, "She sees the good things people do, however small, instead of being consumed by the bad stuff that can be enragingly conspicuous. By embracing the good, she finds the passion she needs to fight for it. Then others catch the spirit and great things happen."

Since June is both a journalist and an activist, it's not surprising that she has also written many provocative books about important social issues. After *Twelve Weeks in Spring* and *Jim: A Life with AIDS*, she wrote *Trial Without End: A Shocking Story of Women and AIDS*. The book detailed how

Charles Ssenyonga lied about having AIDS and deliberately put women at risk to catch the deadly disease. *Trial Without End* showed June's compassion, as well as her abiding interest in legal proceedings. In the introduction she wrote, "It is important to tell the story of Charles Ssenyonga and of the frustration that met every effort to stop his behavior... I hope that this book will help spread the word that AIDS can happen to anyone."

Another legal case she explored, in *The Sleepwalker*, was the trial of Ken Parks, who drove across town and murdered his mother-in-law, and then said he was innocent because he was actually asleep the whole time. His defense sounded absurd, but medical consultants concluded that he had indeed been sleepwalking and really didn't know what he was doing. Ken Parks was acquitted. It was the first time a sleepwalking defense had been used in a murder trial in Canada.

June is also fascinated by history, and by people's individual stories. After about 10 years of research and writing, she published *Portrait of Canada*. In this book, which wryly tries to explain Canada to Canadians (and may be to a few Americans who might listen), she declares, "It isn't true that Canadians don't care about Canada. Canadians dislike (a) other Canadians, and (b) their governments, but will fight to the death if either is threatened." She also notes the curious relationship between Canadians and Americans. "In a clutch, an American goes for a gun; a Canadian calls the police, who arrive promptly and in great numbers." All the same, "Pressed by the weight of ice and rocks at their backs, most Canadians live as close to the American border as they can without changing citizenship." June could appreciate the irony that this history book about Canada was published by an American publisher.

June interviewed some fascinating people on her show for Vision TV during the 1990s. She compiled some of the interviews into another book (named after the show), *June Callwood's National Treasures*. She was in her late sixties when the series began, but she refused to wear makeup on the air. She said, "Old women appear on television mainly as props in commercials about tea or dentures. I hoped my weathered face and sagging jawline would make it easier for other old women to surmount the barriers." It worked. People wanted to hear what she and guests like writer Farley Mowat and ballerina Karen Kain said, instead of paying attention to their age or their appearance.

In 2000 June published a book called *The Man Who Lost Himself: The Terry Evanshen Story*, about a former football star who was involved in a terrible traffic accident. Another driver went through a red light and hit Terry's Jeep broadside. Terry suffered such serious brain injuries that he was never the same again. He lost his memory, his physical abilities, his sense of humor—even his sense of smell. But after years of painful rehabilitation, he managed to regain some of his abilities and he now gives talks to high-school students. Terry Evanshen's story must have had a powerful impact on June because of Jill's accident, Brant's operation, and Casey's death.

In addition to her 30 books, June has written approximately 1,500 articles, on a wide variety of topics, for magazines including *Chatelaine, Homemaker's, Maclean's, Canadian Living, Toronto Life,* and *Reader's Digest*—as well as newspapers such as *The Brantford Expositor* and the *Globe and Mail*.

One of her favorite articles is "The Day the Iroquois Flew," about the powerful engine that was being designed for the Avro Arrow. The writing was technically difficult, and she enjoyed the challenge of being in an all-male environment of test pilots, designers, and engineers. Here's the beginning of that article:

> The big plane hung low under listless cloud, a freak aircraft that induced pity for its awkwardness. Basically it was still a medium bomber, the B-47, with six jet engines streaming black smoke, but aeronautical engineers had warped its shark outline. Clamped to one side of its tail was a seventh engine, the two-ton Iroquois, which has been called the most powerful jet engine in the world.

June even dipped a toe into Trent's lake, and wrote about sports. In 1959 she wrote "The Maurice Richards," about Quebec hockey superstar "Rocket" Richard and his family. She said, "Although Richard won the MVP (most valuable player) trophy only once, he is known as one of the fiercest competitors ever to lace up skates." Richard was suspended for hockey violence in March 1955, for the remainder of the season. His suspension led to one of the worst sports riots in Canada's history.

But of course her busy writing career hasn't been enough for June Callwood. She has been a patron or advisory board member for more than 60 organizations, a judge for more than 23 awards, and has been active in more than 80 professional and community organizations, including the Canadian Civil Liberties Association, the Toronto Arts Council, and the Writers' Union of Canada. Over the years, her contributions have been recognized by organizations all over Canada. Seventeen universities have given her an honorary doctorate (a degree given as an honor rather than as the result of academic work). Not bad for someone who never finished high school!

But in a way, she did. Argyle Alternative High School is a school in Winnipeg where people who have dropped out of high school can go back to finish their education. Because June never completed high school, the students asked their principal if they could give her an honorary high-school diploma. He enthusiastically agreed. In 1993, June stood up to receive that diploma, along with eight or nine streetwise kids sporting tattoos and blue-dyed hair. It was one of the proudest moments of her life. That high-school diploma still hangs on her office wall.

Among June's many other awards are the Order of Canada, three times—the "complete set," she gleefully told Adrienne Clarkson, the Governor General who presented her with the third one. That means she was named a Member in 1978, an Officer in 1986, and a Companion—the highest rank—in 2001. The Toronto Arts Foundation gave her its Lifetime Achievement Award in 1990, as did the Canadian Journalism Foundation in 2004.

But a house only has room for so many trophies and certificates, so it was fortunate that the City of Toronto decided to honor June in two rather different ways. A street in the Queen and Broadview neighborhood

has been named June Callwood Way, and June has also had a park in the new Fort York development named after her. In an interview at the time, June said she looked forward to rounding up her grandchildren and having a picnic in *her* park. In typical fashion, she added, "I'd like children in my park, especially little ones. I'd like places for little ones to be comfortable." She remains very clear about her philosophy of life: "The only way to make the world safer for yourself is to treat other people well. It takes hard work and thoughtfulness. Be brave. Give everything a try if it isn't harmful to others."

Although other people have called June Callwood a saint, she doesn't see herself as one. She is someone who has worked hard her whole life to help the poor, the homeless, the dying—people on the fringes of society. In spite of her troubled adolescence, in spite of not having a lot of formal education, and in spite of experiencing more sorrow than most people could bear, June Callwood has made a real difference in the world.

From top to bottom, left to right:
June with Dr. Phil Berger, one of Toronto's first AIDS doctors; Clowning with Raffi; June with author Jean Little;
June and Al Purdy; at the piano with "Honest" Ed Mirvish; June with: Ruth Grier; Knowlton Nash; Frank Shuster; Herb Whittaker; and Pierre Berton, Elspeth Cameron, Don "Charlie Farquharson" Harron, and Margaret Atwood

EPILOGUE

IN NOVEMBER 2003, June was diagnosed with inoperable cancer. She decided not to undergo any treatment; in fact, she said she was pleased that she would soon "be out of here."

Why did this strong, determined woman react this way to such overwhelming news? "I don't like dependency. I'm just not going to be good at that. I hate the thought that I'd be taking people away from the things they really need to do."

That sounds reasonable—until you remember that the things June herself has "really needed to do" have always been for *other people*. She is a model for all of us, and an inspiration. Even when June herself is gone, her candle will glow for a very, very long time.

TIMELINE

1924   Born in Chatham, Ontario, June 2.

1926   Moves to Belle River, Ontario.

1934   Moves to Kitchener; attends Victoria Public School for two years.

1936   Attends Notre Dame Academy (in Waterdown, near Hamilton).

1937   Attends Kitchener-Waterloo C.I. and Vocational School.

1939   Moves to Regina, Saskatchewan; attends Regina Central Collegiate.

1940   Moves to Brantford, Ontario; attends Brantford C.I.

1941   Quits school; works for *The Brantford Expositor*.

1942   Moves to Toronto, Ontario; works for the *Globe and Mail*.

1943   Marries Trent Frayne.

1946   Takes flying lessons with Violet Milstead.

1957	Ghostwrites first book with Dr. Marion Hilliard.
1964	Writes first book under own name: *Love, Hate, Fear & Anger*.
1968	Founds Digger House.
1973	Founds Nellie's Hostel for Women.
1975–78	Writes as columnist for the *Globe and Mail*.
1980	Daughter Jill is seriously injured in an accident.
1982	Jessie's Centre for Teenagers opens.
1982	Son Casey is killed.
1983–1989	Writes as columnist for the *Globe and Mail*.
1988	Casey House opens.
1991	Resigns from Nellie's.
1990s	Hosts "Callwood's National Treasures" on Vision TV.
1991	Takes gliding lessons.
1991	Son Brant has a serious operation.
2003	June is diagnosed with cancer.
2004	City of Toronto announces creation of June Callwood Way.
2005	June Callwood Park is named.

SELECTED ORGANIZATIONS

Chair of the Writers' Union of Canada, a national organization that brings writers together to help them advance their collective interests.

President of the Canadian Centre PEN International, the Canadian branch of an international association of writers and supporters formed to defend the right of freedom of expression, and to raise awareness of that right. International PEN assists writers around the world who have been persecuted or exiled for expressing their thoughts.

1985–89   Director of the Toronto Arts Council, a funding body that supports the development, accessibility, and excellence of the arts in Toronto.

1995–96   Chair of the Book and Periodical Council, an umbrella organization for groups involved in writing, editing, publishing and manufacturing, distribution, selling, and lending books and periodicals in Canada.

1964–88   Vice-President of the Canadian Civil Liberties
           Association, a non-profit organization dealing with legal
           issues of civil liberties and human rights.

1987–91   Lay Bencher for the Law Society of Upper Canada.
           (A lay bencher is not a lawyer but is appointed to help
           oversee the work of the Law Society, the professional
           organization of Ontario lawyers. Part of June's job was to
           review complaints against lawyers brought by clients. She
           also chaired a committee to improve the Law Society's
           complaints procedures.)

1982–3,
1987–9   President of Jessie's Centre for Teenagers.

1974–79   President of Nellie's Hostel for Women.

1988, 1992 President of Casey House Foundation.

1997–   Co-Chair of the Campaign Against Child Poverty.

SELECTED HONORS

1969   B'nai B'rith Woman of the Year.

1974   City of Toronto Award (the highest civilian award given
        by the city).

1978   Member, Order of Canada.

        First honorary doctoral degree, University of Ottawa.

1984   Order of the Buffalo Hunt, Manitoba (given for
        "excellence in achievement within our society").

        Canadian News Hall of Fame.

1986   Officer, Order of Canada.

1990   Lifetime Achievement Award, Toronto Arts Foundation.

1993	Honorary High School Diploma, Argyle High School, Winnipeg, Manitoba.
2001	Companion, Order of Canada.
2002	Harmony Award, Harmony Movement, in "recognition of an individual or organization that has made a significant contribution towards eliminating barriers to diversity in Canada."
2004	Lifetime Achievement Award, Canadian Journalism Foundation. Toronto Humanist of the Year, given by the Humanist Association of Toronto, an organization that promotes secular humanism.
2005	Jane Jacobs Lifetime Achievement Award, given by the Canadian Urban Institute, an organization that aims to enhance the quality of life in urban areas in Canada and internationally. Thérèse Casgrain Volunteer Award, given by Social Development Canada to a person who has shown a lifelong commitment to volunteering.

June Callwood and Jane Jacobs on the front page of the *Toronto Star* on May 25, 2005.

Liberals finally catch breaks

A by-election goes their way, a wayward MP hints at her return and an audit fails to find a smoking gun

SUSAN DELACOURT
OTTAWA BUREAU CHIEF

OTTAWA—After weeks of pummelling by the opposition, Prime Minister Paul Martin's Liberals got a light, late-spring shower of good news.

Five days after narrowly escaping the defeat of his government, Martin's team got a boost yesterday from Liberal Todd Russell's win in a by-election in Labrador.

And contrary to predictions that an auditor's report released at the Gomery commission yesterday would expose new levels of corruption by Liberals, the party was largely unscathed.

On top of this, independent MP Carolyn Parrish said the door may be opening to return her to the Liberal caucus — although not immediately.

It means that a government on the verge of collapse last Thursday was able to breathe some cautious relief yesterday, even as all political parties were taking advantage of the current parliamentary break to regroup.

➤ Please see Liberals, A7

➤ More coverage of the Liberals' fortunes, A6-A7

NOT A BAD LITTLE DAY FOR PAUL MARTIN'S PARTY

AUDITORS GO EASY
An auditors' report tabled at the Gomery commission inquiry into the Liberal sponsorship scandal lets the party off easy, with no proof of cash payments.

PARRISH PONDERS RETURN
Independent MP Carolyn Parrish is considering returning to the Liberals after talking to Prime Minister Paul Martin — but only after Gomery reports later this year.

GREWAL'S STORY MAY FIZZLE
Tory MP Gurmant Grewal, who charged last week the Liberals offered him a job in exchange for his vote, has a history of similar accusations, dating back to 1995.

BY-ELECTION BOOST
Liberal Todd Russell's win in the Labrador by-election gives the Liberals one more vote in the House of Commons, perhaps ensuring safe passage for Martin until next year.

Urban legend Jane Jacobs gives city planners a dressing down

RENÉ JOHNSTON/TORONTO STAR

Jane Jacobs, left, and June Callwood embrace at the Fairmont Royal York hotel yesterday. Jacobs presented a lifetime achievement award to Callwood for public service.

A mess in our backyard?

Citizens getting ignored, planners told
Councillor, mayor say changes coming

JOHN SPEARS
CITY HALL BUREAU

Toronto's planners favour developers over citizens, says urban affairs guru Jane Jacobs.

Called to give the Canadian Urban Institute award that bears her name, Jacobs stood before a room full of urban planners and policy-makers and harshly criticized Toronto's planning process.

"If citizens don't like it, you call them names (and say) that they're selfish and ignorant and that they're NIMBY — not in my backyard," Jacobs told planners.

"It's true that people don't want certain things in their backyard," she said. "But they're usually right.

"The (Toronto) planning department is really the North York planning department."

Planners routinely smooth the way for developers, she told the audience at the Fairmont Royal York hotel where she presented the Jane Jacobs Lifetime Achievement Award to author

➤ Please see Urban, A8

➤ June Callwood lauded, B5

➤ Royson James's view, B1

'We've got to get back to a planning department that is responsive to citizens, and not just to itself and developers'

Jane Jacobs,
urban affairs expert

Mohammed at home becomes Mo at school

Teens 'torn,' Peel study shows

Sex, drugs among habits examined

TESS KALINOWSKI
EDUCATION REPORTER

They have sex before they're 16, eat candy instead of veggies and don't floss. It's official: Teenagers in Peel Region are just as likely to endanger their health as kids in the rest of Ontario.

This has come as a surprise to some Peel health officials, who had speculated that the influx of recent immigrants to the region might have a bearing on the health habits of its youngsters.

The statistics, an eye-opener for any parent, will likely come as a jolt to new Canadians, who suffer culture shock much longer than their youngsters, say immigration and education experts.

But the data on teen health habits — from sex and drugs to sunscreen and bike helmets — could be the hard numbers to confront some community groups and parents, who don't or won't acknowledge their teenagers' behaviour, said Naima Adan, an outreach worker with the Multicultural Interagency Group of Peel.

"Kids are torn between what they're assimilated into and their home, which is very backward to them," she said.

Mohammed at home becomes Mo at school. And parents who have been raised to treat sex as taboo may be afraid to open the Pandora's box, even if they suspect their children are sexually active.

➤ Please see Youth, A9

Cutting-edge cancer knife

The revolutionary 22.5-tonne Gamma Knife has been added to the cancer-fighting arsenal at Toronto Western Hospital. Story, A3

Complete Index, A2

Ellie **D2**	Classified **D4**
Births **B7**	Editorials **A18**
Deaths **B6**	Horoscope **D2**
Comics **F8**	TV listings **B8**
Crossword **F7**	Weather **B8**

Store and Box Price Monday to Friday 70¢ + 5¢ GST = 75¢ (higher outside the GTA)

7 71412 00003 1

TSO world premiere of Star Wars Concert

Narrated story to accompany music
Actor who plays C-3PO will star

MARTIN KNELMAN
ENTERTAINMENT COLUMNIST

You've seen all six *Star Wars* movies, most of them more than once. You bought the CDs of the movie soundtracks, and your closets are full of old *Star Wars* toys.

But what can you do now that George Lucas has pulled the plug and insisted that there will be no more instalments after *Episode III – Revenge of the Sith*, which opened last week and is currently shattering box office records?

Well, there's one more *Star Wars* experience coming up. The *Star Wars* Concert will have its world premiere at Roy Thomson Hall with two concerts on June 28 and 29, starring the Toronto Symphony Orchestra and the British actor who plays C-3PO.

It's the creation of Erich Kunzel, the 70-year-old music director of the Cincinnati Pops Orchestra.

➤ Please see Star Wars, A16

2006   June Callwood Professorship in Social Justice, Victoria College, Toronto. This endowment allows a professor to teach one course in social justice every year.

Canadian Library Association Advancement of Intellectual Freedom Award, given to a person who shows leadership and courage in defending intellectual freedom and resisting censorship in Canada.

Right: Governor General Jules Léger makes June a Member of the Order of Canada in 1978.

Opposite top left: June, third from left, at the ceremony for the YWCA's Women of Distinction Award in 1986

Opposite top right: June's last day as Lay Bencher for the Law Society of Upper Canada

Opposite bottom: June receives her first honorary degree from the University of Ottawa in 1978.

June was made an Officer, Order of Canada, by Governor General Jeanne Sauvé in 1986.

SOURCES OF QUOTES

Information about June Callwood's books and videos appears in the bibliography.

Epigraph
Callwood, "Each person is like a stone," in Rick McConnell, "Activist focuses on hope," *Edmonton Journal*, Feb. 6, 1996, C4.

Introduction
Rona Maynard, "master of the art of hope," in "Changing the world: How hope can make all the difference," *Chatelaine*, Jan. 1995, p. 24.

Chapter 1
Callwood, "I was a loner," in e-mail to author, Aug. 2, 2006.
Callwood, "Drenched in shame," in *Dropped Threads 3: Beyond the Small Circle*, edited by Marjorie Anderson (Toronto: Vintage Canada, 2006), p. 366.

Chapter 2
Callwood, "It all flooded back," in Rory Sweeting, "Journalists can be activists too," *Toronto Observer*, Jan. 17, 2003.
Callwood, "black fathomless sky," in "Starry, Starry Nights," *Homemaker's*, Summer 1996, p. 58.
Callwood, "sewing hundreds of tiny sequins," in e-mail to author, Aug. 2, 2006.
Leonard Levy, "The guys in the bomb-disposal squad," in conversation with author, May 17, 2006.
Ross McLean, "June was unlike anyone we had known," in "Happy 16th... uh, 60th to you, June," *Globe and Mail (Broadcast Week)*, June 2–8, 1984, p. 11.

Callwood, "Miss Raymond was a perfect character," in Susan Crean, *Newsworthy: The Lives of Media Women* (Toronto: Stoddart, 1985), p. 30.

Chapter 3
Callwood, "It took a Canadian pilot," in "Eight long weeks," *Globe and Mail*, Aug. 26, 1944, p. 13.
Callwood, "In the manner of the old fox," in "Look Like Magazine Cover for $30 in N.Y. Styles Now," *Globe and Mail*, Aug. 20, 1945, p. 10.
Callwood, "Fashions for the algebra," in "Bobby Socks, Sloppy Dress 'Out,' Style Show Reveals," *Globe and Mail*, Jan. 23, 1946, p. 10.
Callwood, "I was still in my teens," in letter to author, Oct. 6, 2004.
Crean, "She made it because she was clever," *Newsworthy*, p. 32.

Chapter 4
Trent Frayne, "I was an only child," *Tales of an Athletic Supporter* (Toronto: McClelland & Stewart, 1990), p. 64–65.
Trent Frayne, "I had to write my copy," *Tales of an Athletic Supporter*, p. 68.
Pierre Berton, "likely Canada's greatest," in Leslie Scrivener, "Portrait of a Marriage," *Toronto Star*, Dec. 2, 1990, D1.
Jack Batten, "He builds humor into it," in interview with author, Aug. 4, 2005.
Trent Frayne, "The millennium beckons," in "Lionel Conacher," *CARP News*, June 1999.
Callwood, "He's a lovely-looking person," in *Person 2 Person* interview with Paula Todd (Toronto, TVOntario, Oct. 2004).
Trent Frayne, "gorgeous, long-legged and sweet," in Scrivener, "Portrait of a Marriage."
Trent Frayne, "Honey, if you want," *Person 2 Person*, Oct. 2004.
Callwood, "Because of the family bond," in *Click: Becoming Feminists*, edited by Lynn Crosbie (Toronto: Macfarlane Walter & Ross, 1997), p. 131.

Chapter 5
Callwood, "Two nights a week," in "Bell's Sweet Singers," *Maclean's*, June 15, 1947, p. 13.
Callwood, "quirky, funny old house," in interview with author, Nov. 24, 2004.
Callwood, "I would have had a baby," in *Man Alive* interview with Roy Bonisteel, CBC TV, Nov. 15, 1988.

Callwood, "After living through the Depression," in "Requiem for a dream," *Maclean's*, Jan. 13, 1997, p. 56.

Jill Frayne, "My parents worked at home," in "Jill Frayne outdoors," www.womenspost.ca.

Jesse Frayne, "For us, there was a great deal," in Scrivener, "Portrait of a Marriage."

Robert Collins, "And there was June," in *Who He?: Reflections on a Writing Life* (Vancouver: Douglas & McIntyre, 1933), p. 36.

Robert Fulford, "June wrote with dash," in interview with author, June 16, 2005.

Callwood, "The day that sixteen-year-old," in "How Marilyn Swam the Lake," *Maclean's*, Nov. 1, 1954, p. 12.

Callwood, "What's Out There?" *Maclean's*, April 26, 1958.

Callwood, "How Good Is the Birth Control Pill?" *Maclean's*, July 19, 1958.

Callwood, "The Day the Iroquois Flew," *Maclean's*, Feb. 1, 1958.

Callwood, "It was the most beautiful plane," in "Requiem for a dream," p. 57.

Elwy Yost, "I will always remember," in Brian D. Johnson, "Raising the Arrow," *Maclean's*, Jan. 13, 1997, p. 49.

Brant Frayne, "she is extraordinarily intelligent," in e-mail to author, Feb. 9, 2005.

Robert Fulford, "Callwood has a special ability," in "Who writes the words that laud the lives of the rich, the famous, and the tongue-tied?" *Saturday Night*, Nov. 1976, p. 32.

Chapter 6

Callwood, "the sweet hippie time," in video "Where Have All the Flowers Gone?" (Toronto: Ryerson Polytechnical Institute, 1988). Produced and directed by Karonne Lansel. Archives of Ontario, C96–3.

Callwood, "When I'd been there," in "Where Have All the Flowers Gone?"

Allan Lamport, "Let them get cold and wet," in Michael Valpy, "A refuge for the youthful, mind-broken victims of a sick society," *Globe and Mail*, June 19, 1968, p. 10.

Callwood, "I realized then," in Adele Freedman, "June Callwood's caring yet controversial feminism," *Quill & Quire*, March 1985, p. 73.

David DePoe, "It must really be a drag," in Peter Thurling, "A bagful of bread to pay for a pad," *Toronto Telegram*, Jan. 26, 1968, p. 22.

"We were impressed," letter to Metro Toronto Executive, in "Hippies plan new bid today to establish hostel in Yorkville," *Globe and Mail*, Oct. 24, 1967, p. 5.

Callwood, "I decided I was a church, too," in *Man Alive* interview.

Brant Frayne, "The kids who come here," in Robert L. Gowe, "The hippies move in and neighbors complain," *Toronto Star,* Feb. 12, 1968, p. 19.

Brant Frayne, "Like, I don't lay down rules," in Michael Valpy, "Hippies get message from meetings," *Globe and Mail*, Feb. 22, 1968, W3.

Callwood, "Yes it is," in *Man Alive* interview.

Callwood, "In my generation," in Adele Freedman, "White Woman's Burden," *Saturday Night*, April 1993, p. 83.

Callwood, "there are no innocent bystanders," in *Portrait in the First Person* (Toronto: CityTV, 1970).

Callwood, "hell of the lost kids," in Lotta Dempsey, "A cocktail party shocked into action," *Toronto Star*, July 12, 1968, p. 48.

"Women live in a spirit," www.jwicanada.com.

"We are all very much averse," letter from Nicholas G. Leluk, Council on Drug Abuse, to Hon. Thomas L. Wells (Toronto: Ontario Archives, RG 29–59, July 2, 1971).

Callwood, "I seem to guilt myself," in *Dropped Threads: What We Aren't Told*, edited by Carol Shields and Marjorie May Anderson (Toronto: Vintage Canada, 2001), p. 12.

Chapter 7

Callwood, "Women have different ears," lecture given at Wendy Michener Symposium, *Canadian Culture at the Crossroads* (Toronto: ECW Press, 1987), p. 58.

Callwood, "There's no improvement in the human condition," in *Click*, p. 133.

Zoria John, "Nellie's has a home-like atmosphere," quoted in Lily Nguyen, "Nellie's women's shelter marks 25 years," *Toronto Star*, Aug. 23, 1999, p. 1.

Callwood, "Are you the same woman," in Jean Kavanagh, "Racism charge 'the worst thing ever in my life,'" *Toronto Star*, June 15, 1992, A1.

Callwood, "I was in bad shape," in John Allemang, "The passion of Saint June," *Globe and Mail*, June 26, 2004, F8.

Nazneen Sadiq, "June Callwood's replacement," in "A beige person sees red over Callwood," *Globe and Mail*, June 3, 1992, A18.

Martha Ocampo, "But as long as there is abuse," in Nguyen, "Nellie's women's shelter marks 25 years."

Chapter 8

Callwood, "If you do certain things," in Joan Sutton, "Grief doesn't keep Callwood from CARING!" *Toronto Sun*, June 12, 1983, G21.

Elisa Wilmot, "At first, I felt I was the only one," in "Rebuilding lives of young mothers," *Toronto Star*, June 18, 1989, A26.

Michelle, "When you come to Jessie's," in Adrian Cloete, "Jessie's Centre calm, helpful haven for teen parents," *Toronto Star*, Oct. 19, 1988, A6.

The figures on teenage pregnancy and birth are drawn from Statistics Canada, www40.statcan.ca/l01/cst01/hlth65a and www40.statcan.ca/l01/cst01/hlth65b.

"This is the first place," quoted in Callwood, "Caring teen-aged fathers defy society's stereotypes," *Globe and Mail*, Dec. 4, 1985, A2.

Bonnie, "I often think about how much," in "Jessie's Centre Annual Report 2002," www.jessiescentre.org/whats_new.

Chapter 9

Callwood, "The death of a child," in *Man Alive* interview.

Pierre Berton, "When we hugged his parents," *My Times: Living with History 1947–1995* (Toronto: Doubleday Canada, 1995), p. 328–9.

Callwood, "Whatever the punishment," in Sutton, "Grief doesn't keep Callwood from CARING!"

Jill Frayne, "the sweetest person on earth," in interview with author, Feb. 21, 2005.

Callwood, "Casey had been a regular blood donor," in e-mail to author, Aug. 2, 2006.

Callwood, "People respond in a time of peril," in *Twelve Weeks in Spring*, p. 1.

Callwood, "For the individual who experiences it," in *Twelve Weeks in Spring*, p. 1.

Callwood, "Hospitals were never intended," in *Twelve Weeks in Spring*, p. 2.

Dr. Dorothy Ley, "People with AIDS," in *Twelve Weeks in Spring*, p. 311.

Callwood, "dying is very much like being born," in John Oughton, "Only Connect," *Books in Canada*, vol. 7, no. 6, Aug./Sept. 1988, p. 19.

Callwood, "make sure we got it right," e-mail to author, Aug. 2, 2006.

Callwood, "As in a garrison," in *Jim: A Life with AIDS*, p. 291.

Callwood, "told friends," in *Jim: A Life with AIDS*, p. 308.

Linda Durkee, "They are being fully accepted," in *Sanctuary: Stories from Casey House Hospice*, edited by Patrick Conlon (Toronto: Prentice-Hall Canada, 1991), p. 156.

Callwood, "Neighbors who pass by," in e-mail to author, Aug. 2, 2006.
    "To Casey House and its staff," in Remembrance Book, Feb. 10, 2001.

Chapter 10

Callwood, "being on the edge of bliss," in interview with author, Nov. 24, 2004.
Callwood, "unknotting my soul," in *Writing Away: The PEN Canada Travel Anthology* (Toronto: McClelland & Stewart, 1994), p. 38.
Jill Frayne, "My mother and father taught," in *Starting Out in the Afternoon: A Mid-life Journey into Wild Land* (Toronto: Random House, 2002), p. 248.
Brant Frayne, "My mother had already lost," in "My first death," *Toronto Life*, Sept. 2003, p. 58.
Brant Frayne, "The old Brant," in "My first death," p. 60.
Andrew Murie, "Impaired driving remains," www.madd.ca/english/news/pr /p06jun07.
Callwood, "I live with a man," in Tom Harpur, "Activist Callwood treats life as a miracle," *Toronto Star*, Oct. 19, 1981, D1.
Rona Maynard, "She sees the good things," in "Changing the world: How hope can make all the difference," *Chatelaine*, Jan. 2005, p. 24.
Callwood, "It is important," *Trial Without End*, p. viii.
Callwood, "It isn't true," *Portrait of Canada*, p. ix.
Callwood, "In a clutch," *Portrait of Canada*, p. xii.
Callwood, "Pressed by the weight of ice," *Portrait of Canada*, p. xv.
Callwood, "Old women appear on television," *June Callwood's National Treasures*, p. 6.
Callwood, "The big plane hung low," *Maclean's*, Feb. 1, 1958, p. 11.
Callwood, "Although Richard won," *Maclean's* Archives, www.macleans.ca.
Callwood, "I'd like children in my park," in Megan Ogilvie, "June Callwood Park proposed," *Toronto Star*, Feb. 10, 2005, B3.
Callwood, "The only way to make the world safer," in interview with author, Dec. 9, 2004.

Epilogue

Callwood, "I don't like dependency," in Allemang, "The passion of Saint June."

SELECTED BIBLIOGRAPHY

Books by June Callwood

Love, Hate, Fear & Anger (Toronto: Doubleday, 1964). Revised 1987 as *Emotions: What They Are and How They Affect Us.*

Canadian Women and the Law, with Marvin Zuker (Toronto: Copp Clark, 1971).

Portrait of Canada (Garden City, NY: Doubleday, 1981).

Emma: The True Story of Canada's Unlikely Spy (Toronto: Stoddart, 1984).

A few of June's books

Twelve Weeks in Spring: The Inspiring Story of Margaret and Her Team (Toronto: Lester & Orpen Dennys, 1986). Revised 1995.

Jim: A Life with AIDS (Toronto: Lester & Orpen Dennys, 1988).

The Sleepwalker (Toronto: Lester & Orpen Dennys, 1990).

June Callwood's National Treasures (Toronto: Stoddart/Vision TV, 1994).

Trial Without End: A Shocking Story of Women and AIDS (Toronto: Knopf Canada, 1995).

The Man Who Lost Himself: The Terry Evanshen Story (Toronto: McClelland & Stewart, 2000).

Videos

"June Callwood: A Portrait in the First Person" (Toronto: CityTV, 1990). Executive producer, Moses Znaimer; supervising producer, Marcia Martin; produced by Jim Hanley and Richard Nielsen; directed by Jim Hanley.

"June," on *Man Alive* (Toronto: CBC TV, Nov. 15, 1998). Host: Roy Bonisteel.

Websites

www.caseyhouse.com

www.archives.cbc.ca

www.collectionscanada.ca/women/002026-298-e.html

www.coolwomen.org

www.jessiescentre.org

www.nellies.org

PHOTO CREDITS

Cover
Front: June Callwood with sign:
  Charla Jones/*Toronto Star*
  All other photos courtesy June
  Callwood
Back: All photos courtesy June
  Callwood

Chapter 1
Page 1-12: June Callwood
Page 13: Notre Dame Academy

Chapter 2
Page 17: June Callwood
Page 19 top: Library and Archives
  Canada/C-013236
Page 19 bottom: Ken Bell / Canada.
  Dept. of National Defence /
  Library and Archives Canada/
  PA-169327
Page 20: University of Saskatchewan
Page 22: June Callwood

Chapter 3
Page 26: Used with the permission
  of Sears Canada Inc.
Page 28 top: National Film Board
  of Canada. Photothèque /
  Library and Archives Canada
Page 28 bottom: National Film Board
  of Canada. Photothèque /
  Library and Archives Canada
Page 31: Second Story Press
Page 32: June Callwood

Chapter 4
Page 35: June Callwood
Page 36: Reprinted with permission
  from the *Globe and Mail*
Page 37: Reprinted with permission
  from the *Globe and Mail*
Page 38: June Callwood
Page 40: June Callwood

INDEX

ACKNOWLEDGMENTS

The following people—friends, family, colleagues, and acquaintances of June Callwood—generously gave their time in interviews for this book. I am grateful for their insights and anecdotes: Jack Batten, Celia Denov, Brant (Barney) Frayne, Jesse Frayne, Jill Frayne, Robert Fulford, Jane Labbé (née Callwood), Bev Leaver (Executive Director, Jessie's Centre for Teenagers), Malcolm Lester, Barry Penhale, Edward Shaw (Communications Officer, Casey House).

I am indebted to my fellow writers for their helpful comments and suggestions: Rona (Ronnie) Arato, Ken McGoogan (writer-in-residence, Toronto Public Library), Judy Nisenholt, Rivanne Sandler, Tom Sankey, Judy Saul, Richard Ungar, Sydell Waxman, Lynn Westerhout, Frieda Wishinsky.

My friends and family encouraged me during the research and writing of this book: Meryl Arbing, Naomi Bell, Julia Dublin, Max Dublin, Morris Dublin, Marilyn Potter.

Others who helped along the way: Ron Charach, Jerome D. Diamond, Bill Gladstone, Sister Joan Helm, Julie Kirsh, Danny Krangle, Leonard Levy, Peter Loebel, Tori McCreary, Myrna Ross, Fred Zemans.

This book could not have been written without the assistance of librarians and archivists. Special thanks go to librarians at the Barbara Frum and Toronto Reference branches, Toronto Public Library; archivists at the Province of Ontario Archives; and Sheila Smolkin, archivist at Holy Blossom Temple.

My thanks also to the special people at Second Story Press: Margie Wolfe, publisher; Leah Sandals, marketing and promotions; Carolyn Wood, editorial coordinator; and Melissa Kaita, production coordinator. Last, but never least, my tough and genial editor, Gena K. Gorrell.

Finally, I want to thank June Callwood for her time, her honesty, and her willingness to let me probe into the various facets of her life. She has been an inspiration and a blessing.